RUGBYWORLD

Yearbook 2013

To Victoria Best Wishes [handwritten]

Editor

Ian Robertson

Ian Robertson [signature]

Photographs

Getty Images

G2 entertainment

This book has been produced for G2 Entertainment Ltd
by Lennard Books
a division of Lennard Associates Ltd
Windmill Cottage
Mackerye End
Harpenden
Herts AL5 5DR

This edition first published in the UK in 2012
by G2 Entertainment Limited

EAN/ISBN-13: 978-1-909040-20-5

Production Editor: Chris Marshall
Design Consultant: Paul Cooper
Printed and bound in Britain by Butler Tanner & Dennis

The publishers would like to thank Getty Images for providing most of the photographs for this book. The publishers would also like to thank Fotosport UK, Inpho Photography, Chris Thau and Wooden Spoon for additional material.

CRAFTED

FOR THE

MOMENT

SINCE 1799

1799

GREENE KING
BURY ST EDMUNDS

IPA

HANDCRAFTED INDIA PALE ALE

greenekingipa.co.uk

Opening up new frontiers

Norton Rose Group has global reach

On 1 January 2012, Norton Rose Group was joined by leading Canadian law firm Macleod Dixon. With more than 2900 lawyers, the enlarged Norton Rose Group is a top five international legal practice by number of lawyers with 42 offices throughout Europe, Asia, Australia, Canada, Africa, the Middle East, Latin America and Central Asia.

For our clients this means an enhanced service, increased resources and greater geographic coverage. The new world is upon us.

Norton Rose Group
2900 lawyers
42 offices
6 continents
1 vision

nortonrose.com

Contents

"When buying property
it's all about square feet."

Trainee Estate Agent

Are you living a life without boundaries?

Looking for a new home takes you to buildings of all shapes and sizes – and all kinds of investment opportunities. With HSBC Premier you could be approved for a mortgage to purchase a property at home and abroad. So whether you settle for more bedrooms or more character, the whole experience is a little easier.

HSBC Premier is subject to financial eligibility criteria and is available in over 40 countries and territories.

Your home may be repossessed if you do not keep up repayments on a mortgage or other debt secured on it. If repayments are to be made in a currency other than sterling, changes in the exchange rate may increase the sterling equivalent of your debt.

www.hsbcpremier.com

HSBC Premier

Issued by HSBC Bank plc. Customer Information Service: PO Box 757, Hemel Hempstead, Hertfordshire HP2 4SS. Registered in England number 14259. Registered Office: 8 Canada Square, London E14 5HQ.

AC23509

FOREWORD

by HRH THE PRINCESS ROYAL

BUCKINGHAM PALACE

HRH The Princess Royal,
Royal Patron of Wooden Spoon.

In a year of celebration, we have all enjoyed the opportunities offered by the Diamond Jubilee and, subsequently, Britain's Summer of Olympic Sport. These are landmark occasions and experiences we will only have the chance to see once in our lifetime. However, underneath the high profile of these unique events, the benevolent work of charities such as Wooden Spoon has continued, despite challenging financial times.

I was delighted when Wooden Spoon received the 'Spirit of Rugby' Award from the International Rugby Board just after the 2011 Rugby World Cup. For nearly 30 years the charity has touched the lives of disadvantaged children providing hope, friendship and enjoyment in an environment of understanding and care. This award recognises the wonderful achievements of the rugby community, the regional volunteers and the many selfless individuals who work within the charity to influence the lives of others and, through the game, create a force for good.

Last year Wooden Spoon delivered over 100 fundraising events throughout its regional volunteer network, opened 51 charitable projects spanning 24 regions in the British Isles and has a further 50 projects in progress. At no time in its history has the work of Wooden Spoon been so important and urgently needed.

It is reassuring that Wooden Spoon continues to succeed, despite the harsh economic climate. However, without the ongoing support of business champions and generous individuals alike, Wooden Spoon would not exist. As Patron of Wooden Spoon, I would therefore like to thank you for your interest in our efforts and activities, and I invite you to support this unique and vibrant charity in any way you can.

Anne

Wooden Spoon
The children's charity of rugby

Creating
a Stir For
children and Young People
across the British Isles

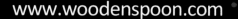

Who we are:

In the UK, one child in every hundred suffers from a lifelong disability that will profoundly affect his or her ability to lead a full and happy life.

More than 3.6 million children grow up in low income households or live in an environment where they are subjected to poverty of aspiration.

Over 1 million young people aged between 16-19 are not in full time employment, education or training.

At Wooden Spoon, we believe that all children and young people deserve the chance to live happy fulfilled lives regardless of the challenges they may face. Spoon harnesses the spirit and values of rugby to give disadvantaged children and young people a chance to achieve their full potential in life.

Wooden Spoon is a children's charity founded in 1983 that is dedicated to helping disadvantaged children and young people across the British Isles live happier, richer lives. We partner with the UK rugby community, receiving invaluable support for our activities and the opportunity to raise awareness of the work we do. In doing so, we involve some of rugby's top sporting role models in making a difference in the lives of young people in need. We proudly comprise of over 40 regional volunteer committees, a central national team and over 10,000 members. All regional committees undertake many local fundraising activities and spend the money raised on projects in their local community.

During our first 28 years, over half a million young people have benefitted from more than £18 million of charitable support thanks to the efforts of our staff and volunteers. We are proud of our legacy, the work we do, and our ambitious plans for the future.

Our Vision:

Wooden Spoon exists to make a
positive impact
on the lives of
disadvantaged children
and young people
through our commitment
to quality charitable work.

IRB Spirit of Rugby Award:

In October 2011 Wooden Spoon was awarded
the Spirit of Rugby award. This prestigious award
recognises the incredible feats that can be achieved
through rugby both on and off the field, and
recognises the incredible fundraising of Spoon and
its volunteers for more than 25 years of work with
underprivileged children across the British Isles.

IRB Spirit of Rugby Award

What we do:

We organise our own fundraising initiatives, raise the money and spend it where it is most needed. Over the years, our donations have diversified from capital projects such as medical treatment and recovery centres, sports and activity areas, sensory rooms and gardens, playgrounds and hydrotherapy pools to include outreach programmes for young people in their communities.

Wooden Spoon has funded hundreds of projects across the British Isles such as:

The Red Balloon Centre in North West London received £40,000 to build and equip a Learning Centre for its pupils who are so severely traumatised that they are unable to participate in conventional mainstream education.

Talbot House School in Newcastle upon Tyne provides specialist education and care services to vulnerable youngsters and benefitted from a £30,000 donation to build a Therapy Suite.

CHICKS Moorland Retreat on the edge of Dartmoor which provides respite activity breaks for seriously underprivileged and deprived children who would otherwise never have the opportunity to go on holiday, received £76,000 to build a new sports hall.

Shropshire Rebels, a thriving tag rugby club for young people with moderate or severe learning difficulties living in the Shropshire area, has benefitted from a £5,000 grant over 3 years to ensure facilities and coaches are available to allow club members to continue their participation in the sport as well as attract new participants to the organisation.

Touch Trust in Cardiff received £10,000 to purchase and install a Sensory Studio Lighting System which enables youngsters with profound disabilities to participate in performing arts-based remedial programmes.

TRY HARD Warrington which aims to help significantly improve the lives of young people aged 16 - 19 who are currently not in education, employment or training across the Warrington area has benefitted from £60,000 of funding for its first year with a target of getting 40 participants through Foundation Learning and back into education, apprenticeships or employment.

Roddensvale School in County Antrim benefitted from a £49,000 donation which enabled it to upgrade and complete an outdoor playground for the enjoyment of its pupils, all of whom suffer from severe learning difficulties.

Wooden Spoon
The children's charity of rugby

What events do we run:

Spoon fundraisers
Spoon's volunteer committees organise hundreds of fundraising events every year including golf days, rugby matches, physical challenges, summer fetes, balls, dinners and many others that raise the crucial funds for the charity and appeal to potential supporters. Much of our impressive growth in members and sponsors is directly related to our event activity.

Spoon Challenges
A series of physical challenges for Spoon that occur across the UK where people can get involved and raise money for Spoon.

The Ford Ranger Great Lakeland Challenge
The longest, highest and steepest challenge. Participants kayak England's longest lake, cycle England's steepest passes and conquer England's highest peak all in just 12 hours.

Four Peaks Challenge
Our most successful and well-known challenge. Participants climb four of the highest mountains in Scotland, England, Wales and Ireland, a total of 14,000 feet and drive the 1,900 miles between them all within 48 hours.

End 2 End Cycle Challenge
On of the most taxing challenges, participants hit the roads on two wheels to cycle the length of the UK from John O'Groats to Land's End, covering 850 miles in just 8 days.

London Marathon
Wooden Spoon has 15 coveted Gold Bond Places for the London Marathon.
Run 26.2 miles for Wooden Spoon in the world's biggest marathon.

The story behind Wooden Spoon:

A wonderful and enduring legacy emerged in 1983 after England's Rugby team was defeated by the Irish. Drowning their sorrows in a Dublin bar, some English fans were presented with a wooden spoon by the victorious Irish to symbolise a winless Five Nations Championship.

Accepting the spoon with as much good humour and grace as could be mustered under the circumstances, the friends resolved to hold a charity golf match to see who would have the honour of keeping the spoon. The money raised bought a minibus for a local school and the idea for a charity was born.

Wooden Spoon Ambassadors - Wooden Spoon enjoys the support of numerous rugby legends and industry leaders who contribute their time and energy to raise awareness of Spoon's activities and help us to generate funds.

Sporting Partners - Wooden Spoon enjoys strong relationships with a variety of clubs, league associations and governing bodies to achieve our common goal of giving back to the community while using sport as a way to improve the quality of life for young people.

Our Royal Patron - Our Royal Patron is HRH The Princess Royal who gives generously of her time.

Our Rugby Patrons - The RFU, WRU, SRU, IRFU, RFL all support us in our charitable work.

Corporate Partners - Wooden Spoon has the generous support of a number of companies whose contributions enable us to grow through our charitable work.

Wooden Spoon, 115-117 Fleet Road, Fleet, Hampshire GU51 3PD **Tel:** 01252 773720 **Email:** charity@woodenspoon.com
Charity Registration No: 326691 (England & Wales) and SC039247 (Scotland)

COMMENT
& FEATURES

Hansen at the Helm
Taking the All Blacks Forward

by RAECHELLE INMAN

'With a short-term contract Hansen is under pressure to maintain a consistent success rate, while also rebuilding to defend the Webb Ellis Cup in 2015'

When Steve Hansen was appointed All Black coach in December 2011 he said, 'I feel humbled and proud to be given the opportunity to lead the team into its next phase. My aim will be to leave the team in a better shape than how I found it and to enhance its legacy.' Given the recent record of the All Blacks, Hansen has set the bar high with this goal. Is he good enough to deliver?

He was certainly the obvious choice to take over from Graham Henry, having been involved with the All Blacks since 2004 and part of the coaching team (with Henry and Wayne Smith) who guided the All Blacks to 88 wins in 103 Tests for an 85 per cent winning ratio. This stint included the all-important victory in RWC 2011 to break the 24-year-old hoodoo; it also included New Zealand holding the prestigious Bledisloe Cup every year, winning the Tri-Nations five times and achieving three Grand Slams against the northern hemisphere Home Unions.

Naming Hansen as head coach allowed for a relatively seamless transition and an opportunity to build on the team's outstanding record. In the search for a potential successor for Henry, Hansen was the only candidate to be interviewed by the NZRU Board and his appointment was a unanimous decision. Henry endorsed the Hansen succession. And why wouldn't he? A good leader designs a successful succession plan. But does Henry's apprentice have what it takes to excel in the top job?

To date, Hansen's coaching career has been mixed. His most significant victories have been achieved in the role of assistant coach, including his seven years with the All Blacks and the two Super Rugby titles as an assistant coach with the Crusaders in 1999 and 2001. His only prior stint as head coach of a national side was when Graham Henry resigned as Wales coach and Hansen, who was his assistant, took over in 2002. He became the ninth Wales coach in 13 years, and during his tenure Wales suffered 11 consecutive Test defeats including losing every match of the Six Nations for the first time in Welsh history. Despite their poor record in 2003, Wales proved to be a surprisingly enterprising side, performing well enough in the World Cup to be competitive against both the All Blacks and England (the eventual winners) but not strong enough to defeat them. Hansen stepped down as Wales head coach in the summer of 2004 after not seeking to renew his contract. Perhaps this inconsistent history was behind the NZRU's decision to offer Hansen a two-year, rather than a four-year, contract. He has to prove he is up to the task of achieving what is expected of an All Blacks coach.

With a short-term contract Hansen is under pressure to maintain a consistent success rate, while also rebuilding to defend the Webb Ellis Cup in 2015. His start at the helm was an interesting one, with two very different results in consecutive weeks against Ireland in June 2012. After a routine 42-10 win over the tourists in Auckland in game one of the three-Test series, it was a very different story for game two in Christchurch. Hansen must have been on the edge of his seat as New Zealand were downright lucky to maintain their 107-year winning

FACING PAGE Steve Hansen (centre) makes a point to Graham Henry (left) and Wayne Smith at an All Blacks training session in Wales in 2004.

BELOW Dan Carter digs New Zealand out of a hole by dropping a late goal to defeat Ireland in Christchurch in June 2012.

streak against Ireland. All Black 'golden boy' Dan Carter booted a dropped goal in the 80th minute to get the home side out of jail 22-19.

Just as France did in the World Cup final in 2011, the Irish revealed the vulnerability of the New Zealand side. Ireland were brilliant and deserved a draw, but the Kiwis managed to steal the win and wrap up the series. Hansen was under enormous pressure the following week from an unforgiving public to restore some pride in the side's final outing against Ireland. In short the world champions needed to get the mongrel back. They needed to win and win well.

'How important is it?' Hansen asks of himself. He knows the answer: 'It's hugely important, it's expected for us to win every game from our fans and ourselves and we wouldn't want to change that expectation.

'What's happened in Christchurch is [done] ... we got a massive challenge from the Irish and we've got to step up to that challenge.'

The third game of the series at Waikato Stadium may have been a 'dead rubber', but New Zealand stood up to the challenge. Their 60-0 demolition of Ireland showed that the All Blacks were back on track. They scored nine tries in their record-breaking win, many of the five-pointers posted by new faces as Hansen used the series as an opportunity to test some depth in the squad.

Dan Carter's injury created an opportunity for both Aaron Cruden and Beauden Barrett to impress at fly half. Cruden has cemented himself as Carter's natural successor. In this match he effortlessly set up tries for a Test newcomer, flanker Sam Cane, and for Sonny Bill Williams, before leaving the field with an Achilles' injury. His replacement Barrett proved he was not overawed by his Test debut as he calmly slotted into the pivotal fly-half position, earning praise from captain Richie McCaw. 'You're always in danger once the score gets to that point that you throw the ball around more than you should, but I was happy with the way Aaron and Beaudy played,' McCaw said.

'They look like they have been there for a while [but] that's because of the hard work that everyone has put in, whether you're starting or on the bench everyone knows what they're doing, and that's what happened.'

Certainly depth in the squad was evident and the future looks bright, with lock Luke Romano rising to the standard of Test-match rugby. Fresh wingers Ben Smith and Hosea Gear both scored tries, while Liam Messam and replacement flanker Adam Thomson also crossed the line in the second half as New Zealand recorded their largest winning margin against Ireland. The previous biggest was 53 points, when the All Blacks won 59-6 in 1992. It was only the third time in their 27 Test meetings that the All Blacks had held Ireland scoreless.

Hansen was relieved that his side were able to dramatically turn around their form from the previous week. They upped their intensity, recycled quick ball and their defence was impenetrable. This 3-0 series victory ensured a winning start to his reign as the new All Black head coach.

One of the nation's newspapers likened Hansen's words after the final Test to an Oscars speech. 'You have got to be happy. It's not too many days you get 60-0,' Hansen said.

'I'd like to thank Ireland for the three-match series, it is a great concept and it's great to once again be able to play a series of international matches against the same opposition,' he continued.

'I'd also like to thank our coaching staff, it's not too often that you get a doughnut, so [defence coach] Aussie McLean can feel very pleased with himself.

'Lastly the players, this week after what was a pretty tough Test the week before, they've bounced back, they've worked hard, were smart, have taken the bullet between the teeth and came out and played a marvellous game of rugby.

ABOVE Conor Murray tries to halt Liam Messam as he makes a break in New Zealand's 60-0 defeat of Ireland in Hamilton.

FACING PAGE Debutant fly half Beauden Barrett, on as a replacement, is welcomed to the international game in Hamilton.

Yet another *formidable* team.

A GROUP OF very different individuals. Each with a specialist skill. Yet all part of the same team, sharing a common goal. Sound familiar? Indeed doggedness, discipline, intense concentration and effort are all elements that are just as important on the Profit hunting grounds as they are on the rugby pitch. If you'd like to find out more about Hunting Profits rather than chasing rugby balls, why not get in touch? You'll find our contact details below. Please remember that past performance should not be seen as a guide to future performance. The value of any investment and any income from it can fall as well as rise as a result of market and currency fluctuations and you may not get back the amount originally invested.

Fig.1: A typical PROFIT

ARTEMIS
The PROFIT Hunter

'We've had the opportunity to introduce some young players, Luke Romano having his first game was very impressive, Aaron Cruden came on and ran the team as if he'd been there for a long time and Beauden Barrett did the same thing.

'So for us it was very pleasing and it was very humbling to be a part of it.'

Hansen said there had been some important lessons from this series and the team had made plenty of progress. 'The key things we've learnt are that if we turn up with the right attitude and the preparation is genuine, by that I mean bone deep, and you don't allow the subconscious to think you've prepared well, then we've got some talent in the side that can do damage to a lot of teams,' he said.

'We've learnt a lot about the players, we've introduced a whole group of young men into the black jersey and by and large we're happy with how they've performed.

'We've brought in some new types of plays and we've allowed those to progress over the three matches and finishing tonight we used all of them and they worked well for us.

'The big thing that has pleased me is that we have also bedded down a new coaching group, including myself as head coach.

'We're a new team that's hit the road and we've hit the road running.

'We're not the finished article; we'll stay humble, keep our feet on the floor and keep working hard to get better.'

While the smashing of Ireland in the third Test of the series was encouraging, Hansen realises that the team needs to continue to improve. New Zealand have never successfully defended a World Cup and he would clearly like to earn the right by convincing the NZRU Board to extend his contract beyond the initial two years.

The game is moving forward at a rapid rate. Does Hansen have the smarts to adapt and innovate at the speed required to stay on top of the competition and ultimately enhance the legacy of the mighty All Blacks? Only time will tell. He will only truly achieve this ambition if he is able to win the first World Cup for New Zealand away from home, defending the title in England in 2015.

Good luck, Steve Hansen!

BELOW 'Blackwash' secured. New Zealand celebrate after their 3-0 series defeat of Ireland in summer 2012.

Aussie's Young Guns
the New Wallabies on the Block
by RAECHELLE INMAN

'Four years ago, Deans was deeply concerned with depth in Australia's back line, now he is comfortable that there is adequate cover across most positions'

It was a high-pressure situation. The Wallabies trailed Wales by one point when the full-time siren sounded. Wales were poised to win their first Test on Australian soil since 1969 after a seesawing contest, but a penalty to Australia on the bell gave replacement five-eighth Mike Harris a big opportunity. In only his second Test outing, the 23-year-old calmly slotted the match-winning goal, clinching a 25-23 victory for the Wallabies. Having beaten Wales 27-19 in the first Test in Brisbane a week earlier, the Wallabies' win from the successful kick also secured the best-of-three series.

As Wallabies captain David Pocock handed the ball to Harris, he said with encouragement, 'Whatever happens, mate, we'll still love you,' and the sharpshooter, who had only been on the field for six minutes, landed the goal from a wide angle 30 metres out. Harris displayed nerves of steel saying he wasn't thinking about the similar shot he missed at a critical stage against Scotland on his Test debut earlier in the month in horrendous conditions, which would likely have sealed that game for the Wallabies. 'It's a kicker's dream to be able to win the game,' he said.

'I've always loved goal-kicking and even for that kick against Wales I was confident. I think Poey [David Pocock] was more nervous than me.

'I just went through my normal routines. I tried to keep my head down through the kick so the crowd knew it was going through before I did.'

Since Robbie Deans took over as Wallaby coach in 2008, he has been on a mission to build depth in the squad. 'We obviously rate Mike Harris. That was a great piece of character he displayed there [kicking the match-winning goal against Wales] … he'll want more,' Deans said.

'Mike has a great ethic, so he will work hard on the things that are required for him to get another opportunity.

'He's a specialist kicker, and he can play 10, but 12 is probably his spot.'

New Zealand born and raised, Harris took a gamble at 21 years of age when he crossed the Tasman to join the Queensland Reds two years ago; but the move seems to have paid off. A former New Zealand Schools and Under 20 representative, Harris performed well in the adventurous Queensland back line in his first two Super Rugby seasons.

In addition to Harris, Deans has identified many new players he hopes will bolster the Wallabies as they rebuild after a relatively disappointing 2011 World Cup campaign. In the first cut of the national training squad in 2012, Deans included 15 new faces – eight backs and seven forwards.

His strategy is to find players with potential, give them a taste of being part of the Wallabies squad and assist them in specific areas. Deans keeps up a regular dialogue with the players so that they have absolute clarity on what needs to be done to realise their dreams of playing top-level rugby. The execution and motivation is then up to them.

'We maintain contact. Anyone who has been involved [with the Wallabies] will walk away with a template with the opportunities we perceive for them where they can make advancements and we keep in touch,' Deans commented.

Deans wants to show the players that the next step is within reach; often it's just the mental leap they need to make. '[With these players] there's a point in time where they're sick of waiting and they start to force the envelope and that's what we're waiting on.'

Four years ago, Deans was deeply concerned with depth in Australia's back line, now he is comfortable that there is adequate cover across most positions. 'We now have a number of five-eighths where we didn't used to have any, so that's good. We're pretty strong through the midfield and we're good on wingers when they're fit. We don't have a lot of specialists at full back but we've got a couple of good ones and some others that can play there,' said the Wallabies' first non-Australian coach.

Deans sees former Australian Sevens captain Bernard Foley as a real talent; the nippy utility can play at either full back or fly half, and this versatility is a real asset to any side he plays for. Foley has the ability to spark something special in attack, especially late in the game when defenders tire.

Deans comments: 'He has good team skills. He hasn't played a lot of 10 for the Waratahs, but he's played a lot of 10 for Sydney University, and he plays well there. He offers flexibility so he's a good bench

FACING PAGE Wallaby stand-off Mike Harris, off the bench for Berrick Barnes, sends the decisive penalty on its way to defeat Wales at Melbourne.

option. He's a guy who could come through quite quickly. He's played some good rugby in a side [the Waratahs] that hasn't been thriving. There's going to be attrition. When you look at the calendar year some guys won't be available for us for the end of year tour [through injury] so there will be opportunities for guys like Foley.'

The 22-year-old Luke Morahan is another youngster who was included in the Wallabies' first train-on squad of 2012. A Wallaby on the 2009 and 2010 spring tours, Morahan completed two non-Test Australian matches prior to his twenty-first birthday, starting his first match at senior level for Australia in the defeat to Munster at Limerick in 2010. He had made his debut for Australia off the bench a year earlier, scoring a try with his first touch during the 31-3 win over the Cardiff Blues.

Like Foley, Morahan utilised the Sevens development pathway as a road to international rugby after excelling for his country in the abridged version of the game. Another adaptable player, he has largely featured on the wing or at full back for the Queensland Reds, although much of his club play has been at centre. 'Luke got his opportunity off the back of some better outings with the Reds; he started to assert himself a lot more. He's always had the talent; he did well through Sevens. He's got speed and a big frame as well. He's just got to learn to use it habitually,' said Deans.

Another new face in the squad is New Zealand-born winger Cooper Vuna, who has made the transition from professional rugby league. 'He [Vuna] obviously has a lot of potential. He also has a fair number of needs he has to address in his game; in particular, accuracy elements whether it be in attack or defence. He's a good lad and he's good in the group in terms of the human dynamics. He's capable of getting it done and he desperately wants to play at this level, so if he takes those steps he offers us an awful lot.'

A product of the Australian Rugby Union development system, Dom Shipperley has made rapid strides on the wing since first being unveiled in Super Rugby towards the tail end of the 2011 competition. Just over 12 months later, the 21-year-old Queenslander has found himself in the Wallabies frame after a compelling run of form during which he has proved himself to be one of the best finishers in the Australian game.

'Dom has had a great Super Rugby series … he has made good steady progress and he has pace which you can't buy, so he has that asset. Dom has shown that he's prepared to work hard and he's made good progress over the last year. He's now a regular starter with the Reds, and he's had a taste with us, so we fully expect him to keep progressing and he'll put the people currently ahead of him under a lot of pressure,' Deans explained.

Another winger Deans predicts we will see more of is Joe Tomane. 'He has a union background, so he's adapted very quickly back into union having had a couple of seasons away. I understand he was a real star at schoolboy level, similar to James O'Connor. We expect him to thrive.'

Full back Jesse Mogg has been a stand-out in the Brumbies back line in the 2012 Super Rugby series; his exciting play earned him an opportunity to be part of the broader Wallaby group. 'He has had an insight. He has done very well on the back of club rugby only and making the step to Super Rugby. He's clearly got the talent, but he's still in year one of training as a professional essentially.'

Deans feels the challenge for these youngsters 'is to play like Wallabies, to play like Test players, week in week out'. And he is watching and waiting for them to prove they are up to the task.

In the backs, the only real area of concern is half back, as there is daylight between Will Genia and his potential understudies. 'There's an opportunity there ... Luke Burgess was a significant loss for us. Will is number one and the others are in the queue. It would be good to have some pressure coming through to keep Will going,' Deans commented. '[Nick Phipps and Nic White] are a couple of good players but they lack the background at international level ... they've both had a taste now ... close to the action and part of the preparation,' he continued.

Deans is pleased that some strong new options have emerged in the forwards throughout the Super Rugby campaign. 'We have a couple of No. 7s coming on which is good because that's an area of need because of the attrition rate. The likes of Michael Hooper and Liam Gill ... Pocock can't play every minute – it's unrealistic.'

Hooper was the 2011 Under 20 Player of the Year and the tenacious open-side has been one of the Brumbies' best performers, consistently topping the tackle count while also proving one of the competition's best ball scavengers.

FACING PAGE Bernard Foley celebrates scoring for the Waratahs against Melbourne Rebels during Super XV 2012.

BELOW On the attack. Cooper Vuna takes on the Wales forwards in the June 2012 Melbourne Test.

He was explosive off the bench in the first Test against Wales in 2012, but nerves caused him to juggle a couple of balls. 'Hooper will never forget it [his first Test] … probably for the wrong reasons in that instance. He's done well, he's only a young man so he's still green. He's got the perfect mentor in Pocock and he's just a really enthusiastic player. He's good on the ball, and he has spent time at the senior level playing in the midfield, so he's got skills and he can play, he can distribute and he has the ability to run and he's quite explosive.'

Having strong No. 7s is a great asset. Typically two wouldn't be selected in the starting line-up, because it would compromise the line out. However, 'it is an option late in the game if you're chasing a game, Pocock and Hooper are both so athletic it allows you to play a different, more expansive game and also to put pressure on the ball if you need ball,' Deans said.

Pocock supported this strategy. 'Having someone who's a specialist at the breakdown coming on when everyone's a little bit tired and the game's opened up a little bit, I think, is a pretty good move.'

There are already high hopes for Liam Gill, who is yet to be exposed to the inner sanctum of the Wallabies. Gill earned a full-time Queensland Reds contract while still just 17 years of age, and in the nine appearances he made during his debut season of Super Rugby in 2011, the young flanker always impressed.

The mobile No. 7 made his Super Rugby debut from the bench in round three against the Brumbies and later made his first run-on appearance when he was selected to go head-to-head with Pocock, Australia's premier open-side player, and the Western Force in round 17.

Liam showed flashes of his talent during that match against the toughest of opponents, although it was a week later against the Chiefs that he flourished, producing one of the best individual performances of any Reds player during the 2011 season. His tireless efforts at the breakdown and in defence were enough to earn the teenager the man-of-the-match award. He also scored his maiden Super Rugby try in that encounter, a pick-and-go effort metres from the line.

'Liam has a good frame on him and he's going to grow into a reasonably big man. He's now got Super Rugby time under his belt so he's ready and able and with that experience mentally he's in a much better space as well. We consciously didn't want to expose him too early for fear of setback. He doesn't have a lot of experience as a line-out forward so that's something we've got to accelerate,' Deans said.

A two-time Wallabies spring tourist, in 2009 and again in 2011, Dave Dennis has been a big improver and a key forward for the Waratahs during the last two Super Rugby seasons. An adaptable forward, primarily as a blind-side flanker but also at No. 8 and in the second row, Dennis was one of the uncapped players named in the Wallabies squad in June 2012, but at 26 years of age he's not a youngster. 'He's arrived in the traditional way. He had some injury challenges early, so he's worked his way through that and he's playing good rugby.'

With Nathan Sharpe's retirement and Wallaby captain James Horwill plagued by injuries throughout 2012, lock is the position that is wide open. 'Clearly there's an opening for someone, so Caydern [Neville] and Hugh [Pyle] are two obvious blokes who will be hoping to get that opportunity, but they're both green, so they've got a bit of work to do. If they get that work done, it's evident that at some point in time they will get access. I am trying to accelerate their development … Sitaleki Timani has a head start on those two.'

Just three years ago Caydern Neville was an Australian Institute of Sport rower; a sport in which he represented Australia at the Youth Olympics. He set out looking for a new challenge and took up rugby, starting on the bench for Manly Marlins' fourth grade in the Sydney club game. Neville's 2.02m (6ft 7½in) and 120kg (18st 12½lb) frame, and an aggressive attitude, made him a quick success at Manly, and this year he won a contract at the Melbourne Rebels.

After having played only three Super Rugby games, Neville was the bolter in the 39-man Wallaby training squad announced in June. While he did not play in any of the Tests against Scotland and Wales, he will almost certainly tour Europe with the Wallabies at the end of the year. And after getting some experience as part of the Wallabies train-on camp, Neville is keen to have more involvement with the national squad.

'It was something that gave me a bit of a boost over the Super Rugby break,' Neville said. 'I learnt a few things, especially from Sharpie [Nathan Sharpe] at the line out and at scrum time. I'm keen to put them into a game situation.

'I guess to be in contention is a great motivating force. It's a great opportunity and you just have to put your best case forward.'

It is encouraging for Australian rugby that there is good depth in the ranks of potential Wallabies, with several exciting young prospects under Robbie Deans's tutelage. The challenge for Deans is to bring that abundance of raw talent to fruition in creating top-quality Wallabies in the future. It remains a work in progress.

> **BELOW** Replacement flanker Dave Dennis secures line-out ball as Australia squeeze home 20-19 against Wales at Sydney in the third Test of the 2012 tour.

1888 And All That
125 Years of the Lions

by CHRIS THAU

'Overall it was a very successful tour, though opinion regarding the beneficial impact of the visitors' playing style on the playing standard of their New Zealand hosts is divided'

At the beginning of December 1887 the news that a rugby tour from the British Isles was in the offing filtered through the pages of several newspapers in both New Zealand and Australia, following a letter from former England cricket captain James Lillywhite. The tour, the brainchild of Lillywhite and his cricket companions and fellow promoters Alfred Shaw and Arthur Shrewsbury, was an audacious enterprise in both sporting and commercial terms during a period of strife in the game. The advent of professionalism had been a major concern for the four Home Unions, at a time when they were at loggerheads following the formation of the International Rugby Football Board (IRFB) by Scotland, Ireland and Wales in 1886. Disagreements between the three Celtic countries and the RFU over representation on the newly formed IRFB led to the cancellation of all matches against England in 1888. Meanwhile, the RFU, led by its redoubtable secretary, George Rowland Hill, were engaged in a determined struggle to eradicate all aspects of professionalism creeping into the game.

During the previous decade, rugby football had taken the then British colonies by storm, becoming the main winter game there, with the possible exception of the state of Victoria, where the main pastime was Victorian Football – what we call today Australian Rules. This is why the news that for the first time in history a strong representative team from 'home' was going to tour Down Under was greeted with enthusiasm throughout the rugby-playing Empire. The 'English Footballers tour', with Lillywhite as manager, was in every respect a pioneering venture, though a similar project by former Richmond FC and England rugby captain Frank Adams in 1880 had been cancelled for financial considerations.

With cricketing tours to Australia already established as private ventures, the three promoters, Lillywhite, Shaw and Shrewsbury, felt that the time was ripe to take another plunge with a rugby tour. All three were professional cricketers of great renown, regarded as being among the finest of the era, and all three had captained England. By the end of January 1888, the concept of what we call today the 'Lions' appeared in print for the first time, in an interview with Lillywhite and Shrewsbury, at the time in Australia, published in the *Melbourne Daily Telegraph*. In it, the two explained the genesis of the project and the difficulties in securing the support of the Victorian Football Association (the Australian Rules governing body) for the complex undertaking. 'It is going to be just as hot a team as we can get together in all England, Ireland, Scotland and Wales,' Lillywhite said. The main concern of the tour promoters was to secure enough fixtures to enable them to make a profit, or at least break even, given the huge estimated expenditure of about £12,000 (over £1 million in today's money using the retail price index).

Meanwhile the RFU, who had had turned down the request of the promoters to formally endorse the tour, reluctantly agreed to let the players go as individuals, though they warned them against any possible infringement of the laws relating to professionalism. To make sure that the would-be tourists understood clearly that the RFU Committee meant business, one of them, Jack P. Clowes of Halifax, was declared a professional for accepting £12 as a kitting-out allowance. The RFU resisted all attempts to have him reinstated and although he left with the team, he played no part in the tour.

The 20-strong British team, selected mainly by one H. Turner of Nottingham, included five players of international standing. There were four rugby caps: Robert Seddon of Swinton, who captained the party; Harry Eagles of Salford (capped by England in 1888 but did not play an international because their games were cancelled), who played in every game of the tour; Andrew Stoddart, also an England cricket captain, who joined the tour party in New Zealand; and William H. Thomas of Cambridge University and Wales. The fifth international was Dr John Smith of Edinburgh University, who was a soccer cap. There were also several highly rated county players, the majority from Lancashire and Yorkshire, including Charles Mathers of Bramley and Yorkshire and Jack Anderton of Salford and Lancashire, who had played for the North of England in that year's North v South matches, not to mention Thomas Kent of Salford and Lancashire, who won his international colours after the tour. Although the squad was drawn mainly from north of England clubs, it included a few Scottish players from Hawick (William Burnett, Robert Burnett and club captain Alex J. Laing) and Edinburgh University (Dr Herbert Brooks and Dr John Smith, mentioned above), as well as A.P. Penketh, captain of Douglas RFC on the Isle of Man.

The team left England on 8 March 1888 and returned home on 11 November that year. They played a total of 53 matches, of which 35 were rugby games and 18 were games of Australian Rules. They won 27 of the 35 rugby matches, with six draws and only two defeats, though no Test match as such was played. During their stay in New South Wales, Seddon died tragically in a boating accident on the Hunter River at West Maitland, and Stoddart took over the captaincy.

Overall it was a very successful tour, though opinion regarding the beneficial impact of the visitors' playing style on the playing standard of their New Zealand hosts is divided. In an interview with a New Zealand newspaper only weeks before his untimely death, Seddon observed that while there was not much of a difference between individual players, the combination play of the New Zealanders was a bit dated compared with that of the British: 'They seem to play exactly as we did in England two or three years ago ...' he said.

'The style of passing the ball in New Zealand is certainly not equal to ours. Their idea of passing is to throw the ball behind without looking where their men are placed. My opinion of passing is that a man should never pass unless the man he passes to is in a better position than himself, and if he is charged he should turn his back towards the man who does so, and pass with both hands. I have continually drilled into our fellows the necessity of using both hands. The New Zealanders seemed to think that passing with one hand is good enough, but that is a mistake.'

T.R. Ellison, meanwhile, a leading member of the 1888 New Zealand Natives team and captain of New Zealand in 1893, claimed in his book *The Art of Rugby Football* that the 1888 English Footballers tour had minimal, almost inconsequential impact on New Zealand rugby. His view was challenged by two of the finest New Zealand players and captains of the 20th century, Dave Gallaher and J.W. Stead, the captain and vice-captain of the 1905 'Originals': 'It was left to Stoddart's British team to show Maoriland the fine points of the Game and the vast possibilities of combination. The exhibitions of passing

which they gave were most fascinating and impressive to the New Zealander, who was not slow to realise the advantages of these methods. One may safely say that, from that season, dates the era of high-class rugby in the colony.'

With hindsight, the assessment of Gallaher and Stead seems more accurate, matching the pertinent points raised by Seddon rather than the dismissive notes of Ellison. Undoubtedly 1888 became a seminal year in the history of the game, as rugby tours, pioneered by Australian teams crossing the Tasman Sea as early as 1882, became not only the means of transfer of know-how and innovation but also essential pieces in the edifice of the game worldwide. Tours secured the prosperity of the game in the hosting unions while spreading the rugby 'gospel' far and wide. The pioneers of 1888, both the English Footballers and the New Zealand Native Football Representatives, made significant contributions to the unification of the interpretation of the game's rules and practice throughout the world.

In his significant book *Forerunners of the All Blacks*, New Zealand historian Dr Greg Ryan pointed out that for a number of reasons the magnitude of the Natives team's achievements and the impact it had on New Zealand rugby had not been fully recognised. By the time Stoddart's men had returned from New Zealand, skipper Joe Warbrick's Natives had already played 14 of their 74 games in the British Isles. From Britain and Ireland they travelled back to Australia and then, significantly, toured New Zealand again.

'By the time they returned to New Zealand the Native Team had fine-tuned their skills and innovations into a style that would transform New Zealand rugby from nineteenth century folk football to twentieth century national game ... Their brand of sensational running rugby and combined forward play had never been seen before in New Zealand ... They gave a model of skill to guide New Zealand into the future,' wrote Ryan.

BELOW The English Footballers. Robert Seddon is seated fourth from right in the middle row, while A.E. Stoddart is standing second from left at the back.

Long-Range Forecast a Lions Squad to Tour Australia
by CHRIS FOY

'One of the most striking developments was the first trace of doubt about Sam Warburton's previously unquestioned status as the captain-in-waiting for next summer'

Falling off a ladder was a painful accident for Warren Gatland, but ultimately his window-cleaning mishap actually served to facilitate preparations for the Lions tour of Australia next summer. The Kiwi coach of Wales was back home in New Zealand for a spring break, at his beach house, when he fell, badly damaging his heels but not apparently doing any real harm to his prospects of taking charge of the next crusade for the cream of British and Irish rugby. Once the Lions hierarchy had paid Gatland a visit, they were reassured that their desire to install him as head coach would not be jeopardised by the untimely, freak injury.

Gatland was able to fly to Australia midway through his team's series against the Wallabies, for a close-up view of the opposition he will be plotting to conquer over three Tests in June and July 2013. Yet Rob Howley remained in charge of the Wales operation Down Under, thus paving the way for a smoother handover in the autumn and clearing the path to a compromise between the WRU and Lions officials over Gatland's division of duties during that period.

Following his fall, Gatland had to endure a drawn-out convalescing period, which presented an unexpected opportunity for Lions-related scheming even before his appointment to lead the tour had been confirmed. Away from the day-to-day demands of preparing Wales to face the Wallabies, he was able to assess the bigger picture at a time when all the home nations were finalising plans for arduous trips to the southern hemisphere. And what will have occurred to him at that stage is just how big the picture actually is, in terms of the array of pedigree players vying for squad places.

As an integral member of Sir Ian McGeechan's coaching team in South Africa in 2009, the New Zealander gained first-hand experience of the unique demands of assembling a competitive, cohesive, united Lions squad and Test team at short notice. From that tour he will have understood the need for harmony and collective spirit in a party drawn from four countries usually engaged in hostile combat. Three years ago, 'Geech' and his assistant coaches chose an initial squad of 37, and Gatland has indicated that in basic numerical terms he will adopt a similarly streamlined approach – intending to take 35 players, creating real intrigue over selection. Based on the most recent evidence, Gatland faces some monumentally taxing decisions before naming his squad in the latter part of the season, unless injuries cut a swathe through his available options.

When it comes to the perennial political hot potato – the size of each country's contingent – the assumption must be that Wales will provide the dominant faction, in part because they are the reigning Grand Slam champions of Europe and also because their coaches are destined to fill Lions management places en masse once more. Although their tour of Australia brought a chastening 3-0 series whitewash, Wales's defeats were so narrow that much of the optimism surrounding their remarkable crop of talented tyros remained intact.

In a Lions context, one of the most striking developments was the first trace of doubt about Sam Warburton's previously unquestioned status as the captain-in-waiting for next summer. The Cardiff Blues flanker had emerged as a supreme exponent of the open-side arts and then as a precociously assured and authoritative rookie skipper, but injuries kept checking his progress through an arduous season, and against the Wallabies he was a far less imposing presence than he had been so often in national colours, prompting concerns about his fitness. In addition, Wales had an

increasingly accomplished challenger for the No. 7 shirt, in the shape of young Osprey Justin Tipuric.

So Warburton was suddenly on far less firm ground than he had been, but providing he returns to peak condition and prime form, he must remain the captaincy favourite. Two Irishmen who have had the job before, Brian O'Driscoll and Paul O'Connell, are unlikely to be chosen again because of age and frequency of injuries, while Ulster hooker Rory Best, their compatriot, also has leadership credentials but perhaps lacks the clout to accept the responsibility as the figurehead for such a high-profile assignment. England's current skipper, Chris Robshaw, and Ross Ford of Scotland could not be considered on selection grounds.

In all likelihood, therefore, the tour will be led by a Wales head coach – albeit an adopted one – and a Wales captain. Warburton at his best would be sure to claim the open-side berth in the Lions Test side, yet his area of the team provides arguably the most vivid illustration of the conundrums awaiting Gatland. There are at least a dozen back-row forwards of the highest class striving to make the cut to go to Australia, so if all are fit (however unlikely that scenario is) there will be some outstanding players left behind.

At blind-side flanker the choice is staggering, from Welshman Dan Lydiate to the Englishman who wore the No. 6 shirt with distinction during the 2009 Test series, Tom Croft, to Sean O'Brien, the rampaging bull of a ball carrier for Leinster and Ireland. Stephen Ferris of Ulster is a veritable force of nature despite his fragile knees, and from Scotland David Denton's emergence has added another dynamic contender to the mix. Aside from Warburton, there are various options at open-side, with the likes of O'Brien and Ferris able to slot into that position though not out-and-out 'groundhog' poachers. This tour may come too soon for Tipuric, but perhaps not for the marauding Scot Ross Rennie, while a fit-again Tom Wood must be considered a prime candidate to claim a tour place, if he can return to the heights of his debut Test season. Another Englishman, Chris Robshaw, has led his country with distinction since being thrust into the role by Stuart Lancaster, but such is the abundance of back-row class at Gatland's disposal that he may have to settle for a place among the stand-by contingent.

With Jamie Heaslip and Toby Faletau likely to be picked as the specialist No. 8s, five flanker places should go to Warburton and Lydiate, Ferris, O'Brien and Croft, with Rennie poised to join the tour as first reserve. Robshaw is another who could earn a belated call-up, likewise Wood and Denton, with others such as Ryan Jones and James Haskell waiting in the wings if injuries wreak havoc.

The second row is another strong area of increasing competition. Richie Gray, Sale's Scottish giant, is seen as a likely Test starter if he is on song, and Courtney Lawes would provide similar athleticism with an additional edge of abrasive physicality and intimidation. O'Connell, the 2009 skipper, cannot be discounted if his body manages to take the strain this season, partly because Gatland will need a few pillars of experience in the midst of so much callow talent. Wales provide a quartet of possible Lions locks, from Alun-Wyn Jones – a Test starter in South Africa – to Bradley Davies, Ian Evans and the towering Luke Charteris. If Gray, Lawes and O'Connell claim three of the second-row slots, a personal preference would be for the durable, powerful, workhorse qualities offered by Davies to complete a balanced foursome, with Croft able to deputise in the engine room if required.

Further forward in the pack, there is a good clutch of props pushing hard – quite literally – to earn a place. Frankly, such is the dismal state of Wallaby scrummaging, the Lions could pick five uncapped teenagers and still expect to seize the initiative, but instead they have a multitude of seasoned operators ready to turn the screw on the hosts in the set-piece. The two Welsh veterans, Gethin Jenkins and Adam Jones, have experience and remain at the peak of their trade, so they must go, leaving three places available. Despite their own frequent scrummaging problems, Ireland now have a formidable figure at loose-head in Cian Healy, who could even claim the Test No. 1 shirt ahead of Jenkins. Dan Cole has already been Down Under and laid waste to a Wallaby scrum with England and he should go as the second tight-head, with Ireland's Mike Ross and Euan Murray of Scotland in reserve. Another Englishman, Alex Corbisiero, is the ideal candidate to fill the final

berth as he can slot in on either side of the front row to good effect, while also offering a potent carrying outlet.

At hooker, there is less cause for debate, with three places to fill and not such a great depth of contenders. Best is surely the favourite to start in the Tests, armed as he is with leadership credentials and a knack for acting as an auxiliary back-row forward with his sterling work over the ball at the breakdown. Dylan Hartley also captains his club, is a combative player and led England to a draw against the Springboks in Port Elizabeth in June, in the absence of Robshaw. He should go, along with Scotland skipper Ross Ford, with Matthew Rees, who was superb on the last Lions tour, acting as first reserve having seen his Wales place come under increasing threat from Ken Owens.

Behind the pack, Mike Phillips of Wales was a star of the 2009 series and his inclusion is a certainty, but his place in the Test side may not be similarly assured. The challenge should come from two smaller, electric Englishmen – Ben Youngs and Danny Care, the former if he can find the consistency of form which has so often eluded him, and the latter provided his recovery from a period of alcohol-related controversy last season does not run into trouble. That pair possess the pace and off-the-cuff invention to keep Phillips on his toes in selection terms, and the Wallabies alert in match conditions, while forcing the two Scottish veterans, Mike Blair and Chris Cusiter, to bide their time on the stand-by list, ahead of Ireland's Conor Murray.

BELOW Wales are forecast to supply the entire back three for the Test starting line-up, with George North (seen here against Italy), taking one wing, and Alex Cuthbert the other. Leigh Halfpenny would slot in at full back.

Fly half is, potentially, a problem position. Thus far, no individual candidate has stepped forward with a sufficiently compelling case to wear the Test No. 10 shirt. Jonathan Sexton has come closest with his feats for Leinster, primarily, but just when he appears the man most likely, he invariably suffers an off day with Ireland. Yet the primary Welsh hope, Rhys Priestland, endured a collapse in confidence at the end of last season, while Owen Farrell lost his way with England after a stirring arrival in the Six Nations. Scotland's Greig Laidlaw made his

Chris Foy's Lions Squad of 35

BACKS: L. Halfpenny (Wal), R. Kearney (Ire); T. Bowe (Ire), A. Cuthbert (Wal), G. North (Wal), T. Visser (Sco); J. Davies (Wal), J. Hook (Wal), B. O'Driscoll (Ire), J. Roberts (Wal), M. Tuilagi (Eng); R. Priestland (Wal), J. Sexton (Ire); D. Care (Eng), M. Phillips (Wal), B. Youngs (Eng)

FORWARDS: D. Cole (Eng), A. Corbisiero (Eng), C. Healy (Ire), G. Jenkins (Wal), A. Jones (Wal); R. Best (Ire), R. Ford (Sco), D. Hartley (Eng); B. Davies (Wal), R. Gray (Sco), C. Lawes (Eng), P. O'Connell (Ire); T. Croft (Eng), T. Faletau (Wal), S. Ferris (Ire), J. Heaslip (Ire), D. Lydiate (Wal), S. O'Brien (Ire), S. Warburton (Wal; capt)

POSSIBLE TEST XV: *Halfpenny; Cuthbert, O'Driscoll, Roberts, North; Sexton, Phillips; Healy, Best, Jones; O'Connell, Gray; Croft, Faletau, Warburton*

---

own pitch by kicking Andy Robinson's side to a famous victory over Australia in June, but for the purposes of this early selection that will merely serve to secure a back-up role, with Sexton and Priestland taking the squad places in the belief that they have the innate ability to come good at the right time.

The choice of just two out-and-out 10s is possible due to the remarkable versatility of James Hook, who could fly Down Under with the chance to fill any one of four positions behind the scrum – fly half, inside centre, outside centre and full back. However, the Welsh magician's rare gifts have served to cast him all too often as the perfect replacement and that may be the case with the Lions too, for whom he should be placed nominally among the midfield contingent. Two more of that number must be the men who formed such a potent alliance in 2009 – Jamie Roberts and Brian O'Driscoll, providing the latter proves he is fully fit. If he is, then the Irish legend deserves to return to the scene of so many heroics in 2001. He still has 'it': that elusive dash of genius in him – even if the pace has subsided. With Scotland still lacking a real cutting edge in the centre and Gordon D'Arcy apparently declining as a force with Ireland, the remaining midfield places go to Jonathan Davies – increasingly influential for Wales – and Manu Tuilagi. The Samoan-Englishman remains raw and unrefined, yet blessed with such formidable power that he takes some stopping in full flight.

There is ample intrigue in the back-three deliberations too, with the likelihood of six places to fill. If two of those go to specialist full backs (with Hook on hand as further cover), then the top two at this juncture are Rob Kearney and Leigh Halfpenny, who can also comfortably line up out wide and slot long-range kicks to boot. Ben Foden of England could force his way into the mix with a fine season, but for now he is surely the first reserve. On the flanks, George North and his fellow Welsh giant, Alex Cuthbert, have shown the power and prolific finishing which the Lions will need, so they are on course for squad selection, at least, leaving two slots and several candidates. Tommy Bowe was a sensation in 2009, but he has been less effective in recent times, while Chris Ashton blazed on to the Test scene in 2010 and early 2011 but has struggled to impose himself to such an extent of late. Bowe has the edge for now on grounds of experience, but that could change based on form in the coming months. Finally, in the traditions of any Lions squad containing at least one 'bolter', this premature selection includes Scotland's 'Flying Dutchman', the Edinburgh wing Tim Visser. He has been top try scorer in the Magners League/RaboDirect PRO12 for three successive seasons and is another wing armed with immense physical clout. Visser qualified for Scotland on residency grounds in June and promptly touched down twice on his debut against Fiji.

As an indication of just how much thinking and agonising Gatland will go through in arriving at his own final selection, consider this as a XV made up of players not included in this squad – Byrne; Ashton, Scott Williams, D'Arcy, Foden; Laidlaw, Blair; Marler, Rees, Ross; Evans, A-W Jones; Denton, R Jones, Robshaw (capt). That side would be competitive, so the line-up which takes the field for the first Test against the Wallabies in Brisbane on 22 June, provided that injuries haven't decimated the ranks, must surely have a strong chance of laying the foundations for a series triumph.

next

We are proud to support Wooden Spoon Rugby World

www.next.co.uk

INTERNATIONAL SCENE

Investing in Coaching
the European Nations Cup

by CHRIS THAU

'Halfway through the double season, the teams placed first, second and third in 1A gained places at RWC 2011, which used the competition as a qualifying system'

The European Nations Cup (ENC) is the premier competition of FIRA-AER (Fédération Internationale de Rugby Amateur-Association Européenne de Rugby), the organisation that controls rugby in Europe and includes about 50 national unions and federations. Even the Home Unions have become members of FIRA-AER, though the four confine their activity to women's and age-group competitions. Of the 47 unions, 37 are involved in the seven-division ENC championship structure, which operates on a promotion-relegation system over two seasons, enabling every team to play its opponents both at home and away.

The two-season ENC is a huge undertaking of nearly 150 Tests, without taking into account matches played by the likes of Turkey, newcomers who are not yet in the ENC divisional structure. The newly formed Turkish national team so far have defeated both Slovakia (31-5) and Estonia (49-5) and will sooner rather than later be incorporated in one of the bottom-ranked divisions.

The top end of the 37-nation pyramid is Division 1A, known unofficially as 'Six Nations B'. In the 2010-12 competition, it contained Georgia (who ended up champions), Romania, Spain, Russia, Portugal and Ukraine, who finished bottom and were relegated to the second division (1B), to be replaced for 2012-14 by Belgium, that division's winners. Newly promoted Belgium finished the second division ahead of Poland, Moldova, Germany, the Czech Republic and the Netherlands, who drop to the third division (ENC 2A). And so on through divisions four to seven (2B, 2C, 2D and 3).

Halfway through the 2010-12 FIRA-AER double season, the teams placed first, second and third in 1A gained places at RWC 2011, which used the competition as a qualifying system. Under Australian coach Tim Lane, Georgia were in pole position at the conclusion of the 2010-11 round and the 'Lelos' thereby qualified directly for RWC 2011 as Europe 1. Interestingly, Russia, defeated 38-6 by the rampant Georgians, finished second in that preliminary ENC table and also qualified directly for RWC 2011 as Europe 2, while third-placed Romania had to battle through RWC Repechage to secure the remaining World Cup berth.

Lane left Georgia unexpectedly after nearly three years in charge, and former Scotland coach Richie Dixon and Australian defence coach John Muggleton took over, taking the team to New Zealand. Georgia did really well, defeating arch-rivals Romania, while giving Scotland, England and Argentina a good run for their money in pool matches. After RWC 2011 the Georgian Rugby Union started looking for coaches to replace the Dixon-Muggleton duo, who stepped down after the tournament in New Zealand. 'We wanted the new coaches to spend more time in Georgia to work on our high performance and academy structures. Ideally we would like them to stay for four years to include the 2015 RWC,' GRU president Giorgi Nijaradze explained.

The Georgian union went for New Zealand expertise, appointing former Wanganui and Counties Manukau coach Milton Haig as head coach, with Waikato coach and RWC 2007 Japan forwards coach Chris Gibbs and former Lelos captain Ilia Zedginidze as his assistants. Haig pointed out that Georgia had huge potential which could be developed with a bit more structure in both attack and defence. He finished the job started by Tim Lane in style, with Georgia retaining the top position in the ENC hierarchy, despite an upset in the opening match, which the Lelos lost 25-18 to a rampant Spain, arguably the most improved team in the FIRA-AER competition.

Spain, coached by Frenchman Régis Sonnes since 2010, have expanded their recruitment base outside the country to good effect. The 40-year-old Sonnes, a triple French Championship gold medallist with Stade Toulousain in 1994, 1995 and 1997 and forwards coach of Bordeaux-Bègles, identified about two dozen French players eligible to play for Spain, in addition to another half a dozen foreigners qualified to play for Spain through residence. It is true that the number of native Spanish players in Sonnes's starting XV is very small, but he operates within the IRB regulations and the results have vindicated his pragmatic approach.

Spain's considerable progress under Sonnes was confirmed by the margins recorded in their recent matches against Romania, a country they rarely managed to defeat in the past. The Spanish were defeated 64-8 by the Romanians in March 2011, while a year later the result was 13-12 to Spain. 'It is true,' argued new Romanian head coach Haralambie Dumitras, 'that against Spain we have experimented with several new players, including a completely new back row [of] Gorcioaia, Adrian [Ion] and Macovei.

'We had a mixed year, which started with a laboured 15-7 win over Portugal followed by a satisfying 25-0 win over Russia away in Sochi. We started to think that the new approach, the new game we were developing was paying dividends, when the disaster struck. We lost at home 13-19 to Georgia, a match we could have and should have won. It was a catastrophe, from a coach's point of view. Instead of maintaining the approach we used against Russia, the boys felt that they had to revenge the RWC 2011 defeat and took the Georgians on up front. That's precisely not the way to beat Georgia and was everything we had worked not to do, but the instincts are sometimes more powerful than the learned approach. It was awful. After Georgia, I felt that we had no more chances of winning the FIRA-AER competition so I decided to experiment by bringing in new players. That's when the aberration against Spain happened, not that I wish to deny Spain any plaudits. They were better than us and deserved to win,' Dumitras said.

Dumitras became head coach in January this year, the new director of rugby, Lynn Howells, started last December and the new defence coach, Neil Kelly, commenced in February this year, while the two assistant coaches, Marius Tincu and Eugen Apjok, were also in position by February. It was the first time Romania had got its management team up to a full complement, something Dumitras had been battling to achieve from the outset, and former Pontypridd and Wales coach Howells was crucial in creating the right working atmosphere and adding an edge to a comparatively inexperienced coaching team. 'Harry is a quality coach and we became good friends. It is a definite advantage that Romania has got a Romanian coach, but mind you Marius is quite superb and I foresee a great future for him, so is Eugen, not to mention Neil Kelly whose contribution has been tremendous. It is a highly effective team and the fact that we won the IRB Nations Cup just proves that the potential is there,' Howells said.

The advent of professionalism saw the emergence of the complex interdisciplinary coaching/management team of today, much to the chagrin of the traditionalists. In their relentless pursuit of the elusive 'edge', the top-tier unions have evolved complex

---

European Nations Cup 2010-12 Final Tables

1A
Georgia
Romania
Spain
Russia
Portugal
Ukraine

1B
Belgium
Poland
Moldova
Germany
Czech Republic
Netherlands

2A
Sweden
Lithuania
Malta
Croatia
Latvia

2B
Switzerland
Andorra
Serbia
Slovenia
Armenia

2C
Israel
Denmark
Austria
Hungary
Norway

2D
Cyprus
Bulgaria
Greece
Luxembourg
Finland

3
Bosnia & Herzegovina
Slovakia
Azerbaijan

Key
Georgia: champions
Belgium: promoted
Ukraine: relegated

ABOVE Kingsley Jones (front), head coach of the Russian national side, with his management team.

FACING PAGE Portugal head coach Errol Brain, himself a former back-rower, in discussion with his forwards.

management programmes, in which technology and various branches of sport science play an increasingly large role. The high-performance department of the IRB has been providing support to second-tier unions to set in place similar programmes in order to keep up with the big boys. 'It is like a puzzle, a well-structured melange of strength, conditioning, nutrition, lifestyle, sports medicine and specific skills programmes, which are designed to help the individual players fulfil their potential,' observed IRB High Performance Consultant and former Scotland and Georgia coach Richie Dixon.

The other team to benefit from this diverse approach is Russia, whose head coach, Kingsley Jones, has gathered a strong interdisciplinary team to help the side capitalise on its RWC 2011 experience. Jones's interest in coaching was triggered in 1988, while he was still a teenager, during the year he spent with his father Phil, at the time the Counties Union development officer in New Zealand. Coaching seemed to be the right habitat for the young Kingsley Jones, whose leadership qualities had been recognised early by various coaches and club managers and owners throughout Welsh and English rugby. He captained virtually every club and team he played for, from school to his beloved Wales, Crawshay's and Barbarians.

'I was guided by two principles in putting together this coaching team: one was finding the best-qualified people to do the job and the second was recruiting people I knew, able to do the job to the highest possible standard,' said Jones.

'Paul Pook whom I know from my days with Ebbw Vale is a world-class conditioning coach – he worked with Ireland when they won the Grand Slam in 2008. Siua "Josh" Taumalolo, who was Tonga backs coach in the 2011 World Cup and coached their Sevens team, has tremendous experience and I rate him highly. He has played in every position behind the pack and I learned a lot from him. Huw Wiltshire, who is a consultant analyst and was my conditioning coach when I played for Wales A, helps "Pookie" with the conditioning programme and works as well on match analysis. Henry Paul does skills work with the players and is the coach of the Sevens team, while Lions and Wales man Darren Morris is coaching the Russian scrum. Mind you, he got the job by default, as Phil Keith-Roach, the original coach, got injured just before RWC 2011. But the boys warmed up to him so much and accepted his advice gratefully, so he became one of the team.'

In Portugal, with former head coach Tomás Morais in his new role as director of rugby, the main task facing head coach Errol Brain is to develop in depth the elite group currently available for selection. It was a hard season for the former Counties Manukau and NZ Maori No. 8 and captain, being defined by several narrow defeats when a number of his top players were either out injured or otherwise unavailable. This was the untold story of the biggest upset of the FIRA-AER competition this year, when Ukraine recorded their one and only win at the expense of Portugal, who were deprived of 12 top players on duty with the Sevens team. Add to that the unwillingness of the French clubs to release their top Portuguese players to national team duty and one understands the predicament faced by Brain and his coaching team. The majority of the Portuguese players are amateurs and they make huge efforts to keep up with their professional counterparts elsewhere. 'But you can't fault their desire to be among the best,' observed Brain, who has a qualifying berth in RWC 2015 firmly in sight. And division 1A of the 2012-14 ENC tournament, which kicks off in February 2013, is once again an official qualifying round for RWC 2015, with the winners and runners-up qualifying directly, as they did in 2011.

Almighty All Blacks
the HSBC Sevens World Series

by **TERRY COOPER**

'The World Series title gave the All Blacks the commanding heights of being champions at both the traditional game and the quick-fire short form'

The HSBC Sevens World Series is one of this century's unpredicted sporting phenomena – probably overshadowed only by cricket's T20 explosion from nothing. Until the 1999-2000 season, international Sevens was random and unstructured. Hong Kong and Dubai had been constants, and there had been a couple of World Cups. In those days many of the world's major players were eager to represent their nations at either form of the game. Not even a superhero could double-book now, and most Sevens operators are contracted to be just that.

For the past 12 seasons the World Series, spread over half a year and all continents, has produced a genuine champion – usually New Zealand – who needed to slog through several exhausting two-day tournaments. And during the 2011-12 series the teams globetrotted 75,000 miles to the nine venues.

During the May finale at Twickenham, New Zealand claimed the prize for the tenth time in an official World Series. That gave the All Blacks the commanding heights of being champions at both the traditional game – following last October's nerve-jangling Rugby World Cup final win in their own backyard – and the quick-fire short form. But even in their hour of triumph they had to yield the London title to glorious Fiji, who matched New Zealand's mark of three Cup titles in the season.

What a weekend that was! Over the two days 103,027 fans paid their money, even though the hosts had no chance of becoming HSBC Sevens World Series winners. On the Saturday 60,050 turned up, creating a single-day record for any Sevens series. On Sunday it was 42,977. It would unquestionably have been higher, but that Sunday coincided with the final day of soccer's Premiership – good riddance for a few weeks at least.

The huge Twickenham audience hoisted the grand total over the nine rounds to another record – 547,500. Australia's switch to the Gold Coast resort was heavily supported at the start; Port Elizabeth's Nelson Mandela Bay Stadium provided a jubilant atmosphere; and a return to Tokyo was significant for Asian rugby, with Japan preparing to host Rugby World Cup 2019. At three of the venues a women's event was staged – a prelude to a new IRB Sevens series for them.

ABOVE Tomasi Cama of New Zealand, IRB Sevens Player of the Year, breaks through against Australia in Tokyo.

FACING PAGE Twickenham, 13 May 2012. IRB chairman Bernard Lapasset presents the HSBC Sevens World Series trophy to DJ Forbes, captain of New Zealand.

In the future, even the smallest business will be multinational.

Whether you trade in Dollars, Euros or Renminbi, global markets are opening up to everyone. At HSBC we can connect your business to new opportunities on six continents – in more than 90 currencies. There's a new world emerging. Be part of it.

There's more on international trade at
www.hsbc.com/inthefuture

Issued by HSBC Holdings plc.   AC22967

Sophie Goldschmidt, Chief Commercial Officer at the RFU, justifiably delighted at the union's contribution to the mass gatherings, said, 'Setting another record at the London Sevens is a fantastic achievement. That we have been able to set another new high is a testament to the entertainment on and off the pitch and to the strength of the sport, which is clearly getting bigger each year.'

The crowd seem to have been hit by the Queen's Diamond Jubilee fever or even London Olympics frenzy. But there must have been an element of Rugby Olympics relish. You can't play a 15-a-side tournament in the short span of an Olympic Games, so rugby returns as an Olympic sport in Rio in 2016 in its Sevens format, following a well-planned and obviously convincing campaign by the IRB. Well done the Board! Not a phrase used every day in rugby conversations.

Board chairman Bernard Lapasset commented, 'Again New Zealand have proved that, over the course of an entire season, they are the finest Sevens side in the world.'

We kicked off the HSBC Sevens World Series in late November on Australia's Gold Coast, where Fiji began as they finished by coming out ahead of New Zealand, beating them in the Cup final 26-12. Two of the stars of the series, Setefano Cakau and Tomasi Cama, scored the first tries. Cama made it a double by half-time, but the Fijians claimed three unanswered second-half tries for an impressive success. Osea Kolinisau spoke for Fiji when he said, 'We lost to them in the pool stage, so to meet them and beat them in the final was special – truly sweet.'

One week later it was off to good old Dubai – 'a home from home for us', noted England's captain, Greg Barden. Mat Turner, player of this tournament and ultimately the series top try scorer, exulted, 'It's like playing at Twickenham. You run out and the crowd go wild for you. It takes you to the next level and our win gives us the same feeling as last year.' Turner crossed for a couple of tries to take England to a game-deciding 24-7 lead by the interval against France – a rare final without a southern-hemisphere representative – and they eventually won 29-12. England had signposted their marvellous form this week by knocking out New Zealand and Fiji.

Next week, down to the tip of Africa for a new venue in Port Elizabeth, where New Zealand – as they would think – restored the natural order of events, overcoming the hosts 31-26 in a spectacular

BELOW Fiji's Setefano Cakau on his way to the try line against Wales in Australia.

final, with nine tries for the 30,000 crowd. During the final play, New Zealand trailed but burgled the title when Cama successfully pursued a kick downfield for the winner. New Zealand skipper DJ Forbes said, 'That was a bit of a resurrection for us because we defeated all the countries who beat us last week. It's already a crazy series. Pool games have the intensity of knockout rounds.'

The squads were then allowed a break until February, when Wellington welcomed a home triumph. The final was settled in brisk fashion when the All Blacks ran in four first-half tries against a disappointing Fiji. It ended 24-7, and Gordon Tietjens, New Zealand's evergreen coach, observed, 'We love winning our own tournament. There is an expectation when we play at home.'

Across the Pacific to Las Vegas one week on, when swarms of Samoan fans streamed on to the pitch to acclaim last-gasp success against the All Blacks. It was Samoa's first title since they were series champions in 2010. The final was locked at 19-19 when mountainous Alafoti Faosiliva powered over. Emotional coach Stephen Betham admitted, 'It's been a long time. I couldn't stop a tear rolling down my cheek.'

Back to the good old days – Sevens HQ really – with the traditional Hong Kong extravaganza. Where would international Sevens be without HK and Dubai? And Fiji recalled the old times with another title in another shoot-out against the All Blacks. Another big score – 35-28, five tries to four – in one of the great Cup finals of all time. But it was Fiji's first win here since 2009, and captain Setefano Cakau said, 'I thank the boys because it's my sixth time here and it's the first time I have played and won a final.' An important issue was decided at Hong Kong when Canada, Spain and Portugal qualified as 'core nations' and will join the elite in the 2012-13 HSBC Sevens World Series. This was a further expansion of World Series participants from 12 countries to 15.

It became five different winners in seven rounds when Australia muscled in when the circus went to Tokyo in April. Tokyo, of course, will be a major hub when Japan hosts the 2019 World Cup. Wallabies captain Ed Jenkins levelled the scores at 26-26 against Samoa in the final. Matt Lucas – no, not that one – held his nerve and skill to land the wide conversion in the final seconds. Lucas was one of four teenagers in Australia's squad, which hints at a bright future.

Scotland switched their event across the country to Glasgow, where New Zealand swamped England 29-14, skipper DJ Forbes dotting down a couple in the final to mark his fiftieth Sevens tournament. 'The boys told me: "We will do this for your fiftieth."' Coach Tietjens paid tribute: 'What a magnificent captain. Inspirational. He leads and plays outstandingly.'

At last a short flight and no jet lag as the countries hopped down to London. By smashing South Africa 36-0 in a breathtaking, ruthless quarter-final, New Zealand clinched the 2011-12 HSBC Sevens World Series, so they could accept their semi-final elimination by Fiji with about as much equanimity as All Blacks ever can muster in defeat.

Tomasi Cama added to New Zealand's honours by being named IRB Sevens Player of the Year. The Fijian-born playmaker and goal-kicker said, 'It's a reward for the work of all the boys. I concentrate on my game. I control what I can control.' He ended the season with 1627 career points but still in second place on the all-time list, more than 1000 points behind the most prolific Sevens accumulator ever – England's Ben Gollings.

Fiji took the London title with a 38-15 triumph in the final against Samoa. Their coach, Alifereti Dere, called it 'The perfect end. We wanted to improve on fifth in 2011 and now we are second in the series.' It could get better because there were eight players new to World Sevens in his squad.

IRB chairman Lapasset summed up the 2011-12 HSBC Sevens World Series by emphasising, 'The action has been more competitive than ever, with no fewer than 13 teams reaching the Cup quarter-finals.

'In the stands and around the venues the carnival atmosphere continued to provide a unique appeal to fans round the world. It makes Sevens an incredibly enticing prospect as we move close to the 2016 Olympics.'

FACING PAGE England's Mat Turner crosses for one of his pair of tries against France in the Cup final in Dubai.

ABOVE Samoa celebrate a try in front of their own fans during their victory over New Zealand in the Las Vegas Cup final.

Aberdeen Asset Management is proud to support Wooden Spoon and wish them every success in all their upcoming events.

For more information please visit:
www.aberdeen-asset.com/sponsorship

Aberdeen
GLOBAL ASSET MANAGEMENT

Issued by Aberdeen Asset Managers Limited, 10 Queen's Terrace, Aberdeen AB10 1YG.
Authorised and regulated by the Financial Services Authority in the United Kingdom.

2508478

Baby Boks' Year
the 2012 Junior World Championship
by ALAN LORIMER

'South Africa were rocked by a first-round defeat to Ireland, while in the next round Wales caused an equally big upset by seeing off New Zealand'

ABOVE South Africa celebrate after beating New Zealand 22-16 in the final at Newlands to prise the trophy from the grasp of the Baby Blacks.

It had to happen sometime. New Zealand's tight grip on the Junior World Championship since its inception in 2008 was finally loosened as hosts South Africa, playing in front of a captivated Cape Town crowd, rose to the occasion in the final at Newlands to win their first ever title at Under 20 level.

England had shown in the 2011 final in Padova (Padua) that New Zealand were not superhuman by taking the match to the wire but ultimately losing. Not so for South Africa, however, who posted a performance based on massive forward power, tight defence behind the scrum and coolness in the shape of their young fly half, Handre Pollard, one of the undoubted stars of the tournament.

In scenes reminiscent of the 1995 Rugby World Cup, the Baby Boks celebrated in front of 32,000 spectators at the end of a compelling final that had turned on a critical moment just after the start of the second half. New Zealand were leading 10-9 from a penalty by fly half Ihaia West and his conversion of a try triggered by the exciting Southland full back, Martin McKenzie, and scored by winger Milford Keresoma, when they were awarded a scrum five metres from the South Africa line. It was the perfect position for New Zealand to attack and increase their lead, either through their dynamic back row or through their elusive midfield backs.

Neither option, however, came to be used as South Africa produced a trademark scrummaging effort that put the New Zealand eight into reverse gear, earning the Baby Boks a reprieve and a penalty in the process. Minutes later a try by lively scrum half Vian van der Watt put South Africa ahead. Then came a dropped goal by Pollard before an impressive score from the player of the tournament, centre Jan Serfontein, sealed matters for the Baby Boks to give them a 22-16 victory.

Serfontein and Pollard, both eligible to play in the 2013 tournament, to be staged in France, were key performers for South Africa, but the Baby Boks had a number of other outstanding players, not least captain and flanker Wian Liebenberg, fellow forwards Pieter-Steph du Toit and Shaun Adendorff, and centre William Small-Smith, who unluckily missed the final because of injury. In the New Zealand squad, fly half Ihaia West stood out as a future star, along with centre Jason Emery, who caused panic in most defences with his dangerous running, while in the forwards back-rowers Jimmy Tupou and Jordan Taufua look set for further honours.

Neither South Africa nor New Zealand, however, had straightforward routes to the final. South Africa were rocked by a first-round defeat to Ireland, while in the next round Wales caused an equally big upset by seeing off New Zealand, who had beaten the men from the Principality by over 90 points in the 2011 competition. Indeed, Wales, with wins over Fiji and Samoa, finished top of Pool A with New Zealand second, but the Baby Blacks squeezed into the semi finals as best runners-up, thanks to a good points difference. Ireland's defeat to England and their failure to collect enough bonus points left them second in Pool B behind semi-final qualifiers South Africa, and out of the top four. Los Pumitas became the other semi-finalists after three straight wins in Pool C.

Sadly for Wales their semi-final was a rematch with New Zealand; in fact, round four of the championship produced four rematches, such is the quirkiness of the tournament format. New Zealand needed no motivation after their earlier defeat and gained revenge with a 30-6 win over Wales to book their place in the final against a Baby Boks side that had dismissed Argentina.

Wales, disappointed at not being in the final, salvaged pride by defeating Argentina in the third-place play-off, and with impressive performances from the likes of wing Tom Prydie, already capped

at senior level, fly half Matthew Morgan and back-row Luke Hamilton, Welsh rugby looks in good shape. Having missed out on a semi-final, Ireland did not let the disappointment hang over them, and in the fourth round they refocused their effort to defeat England 27-12, before securing overall fifth place with a 18-7 win over France, thanks to six penalty goals from their outstanding fly half, JJ Hanrahan.

After finishing as runners-up in Italy in 2011, Under 20 Six Nations winners England had a championship campaign in Cape Town that fell below expectations. Coach Rob Hunter, however, could perhaps point to the absence of a number of key players, not least Leicester fly half George Ford, the 2011 IRB Junior Player of the Year. It was the Pool B match against South Africa that killed off England's chances. England needed only a draw to progress to the semi-finals, but a four-try second-half effort from the Baby Boks resulted in England failing to reach the semi-finals for the first time since the Under 20 championship was introduced.

ABOVE Fly half JJ Hanrahan (with ball) is congratulated by team-mates after scoring for Ireland their 20-15 Pool B defeat to England. Ireland, though, gained revenge 27-12 in the fourth round.

FACING PAGE Jordan Taufua flies into the corner to touch down as New Zealand avenge their Pool A defeat to Wales by winning the semi-final 30-6.

England finished in seventh position, with a 17-13 final-round win over Australia. Meanwhile, the fourth of the Home Union countries, Scotland, equalled their best finishing place of ninth. Yet it had all looked foreboding for Scotland when they lost their opening match against Australia by 67-12 only for them to regain composure against France and Argentina, to whom they lost just 30-29 and 17-12 respectively. Scotland then demolished Italy and Samoa to finish with the feeling of a job well done. The statistics back this up. Scotland were top in the team try-scoring list with a total of 21, while individually 18-year-old winger Jamie Farndale was the leading striker with six touchdowns and fly half Harry Leonard was second-highest points scorer with 54. Like Wales and England, Scotland have ten of their players eligible for the 2013 Junior World Championship, among them their Clermont Auvergne-based centre Mark Bennett.

Elsewhere France failed to sparkle, Samoa and Fiji survived late relegation scares, while Italy became the unfortunate team to drop from the elite division into the 2013 Junior World Rugby Trophy competition.

Even if the Junior World Championship no more than maintains the enormously high standard set in Cape Town, then the 2013 tournament in France will be well worth watching. Meanwhile, keep an eye on the stars of JWC 2012. They'll be featuring soon on a screen near you.

Summer Tours 2012
England in South Africa

by MICK CLEARY

'There is no such thing as a Springbok side that rolls over meekly in front of its own public. Only a Test series in South Africa can reveal that truth to you'

England were in happy mood as they broke camp in Port Elizabeth on a mild winter's morning in late June. Given the previous day's tidings from Hamilton in New Zealand, where Ireland had been utterly humiliated by the All Blacks, there was a real sense that they had at least flown the flag with reasonable merit in South Africa, bringing further shape to an identity that had been forged during the Six Nations Championship. Tours south of the equator have so often ended in tears and recriminations that you take every little thing you can get. If you emerge unscathed, you're in credit.

The surf was crashing in below England's beachfront base and it only needed a glance at the news from other parts of the southern hemisphere to realise that a young England team might have finished on the rocks (as Ireland had) if they hadn't summoned significant depths of guts and fortitude.

True, it was important for England not to get carried away. They had, after all, only managed one draw in the three-Test series: the 14-14 scoreline in Port Elizabeth secured only in the dead rubber, with the series decided the previous week in Johannesburg. Still, a series victory had proved beyond the Lions three years earlier and it had taken the All Blacks until 1996 to get the better of their arch-rivals on South African soil. You knew, too, that no team coached by Heyneke Meyer would be allowed to coast, to think of battles to come rather than focus on the here and now. For Meyer, every Test is an expression not only of the self but also of the country. It was never to be taken lightly. The Springboks were up for the contest, but, crucially, so too were England.

There is such a thing as a poor South African side, and this vintage has much room for improvement, but there is no such thing as a Springbok side that rolls over meekly in front of its own public. Only a Test series in South Africa can reveal that truth to you, and the benefits of the extended Test programme

RIGHT Springbok hooker Bismarck du Plessis carries half of the England back division over the line with him as he scores South Africa's second try in their 36-27 victory at Ellis Park, Johannesburg.

will be of enormous worth to England as they look to build towards the 2015 Rugby World Cup. Even a two-Test series does not give you complete insight into the mind of a Springbok – that ferocity, that relentlessness, that in-your-face machismo, that rage and pride that propels them to maniacal levels of intensity. England found out all about that in a devastating opening spell at Ellis Park when the series was settled and English minds were befuddled.

That Stuart Lancaster's side managed to get their act together, find cohesion and defiance, and come within nine points of the Boks by the final whistle will stay with them for a long time. What might have been if they hadn't been rabbits in the headlights in the opening quarter; what might have been if they hadn't sat back and allowed, in the words of Mike Catt, 'that big green machine to roll and roll'. Knowing that it's coming your way is one thing; stopping it another entirely. In the early stages at Ellis Park, England didn't manage to; at the Nelson Mandela Bay Stadium seven days later, they did. Recalled back-row forward James Haskell put in a heroic shift of tackling, as did several others alongside. Another man back in an England shirt, scrum half Danny Care, was intent on atonement for sins past as well as on showing that he was going to scrap all the way for that

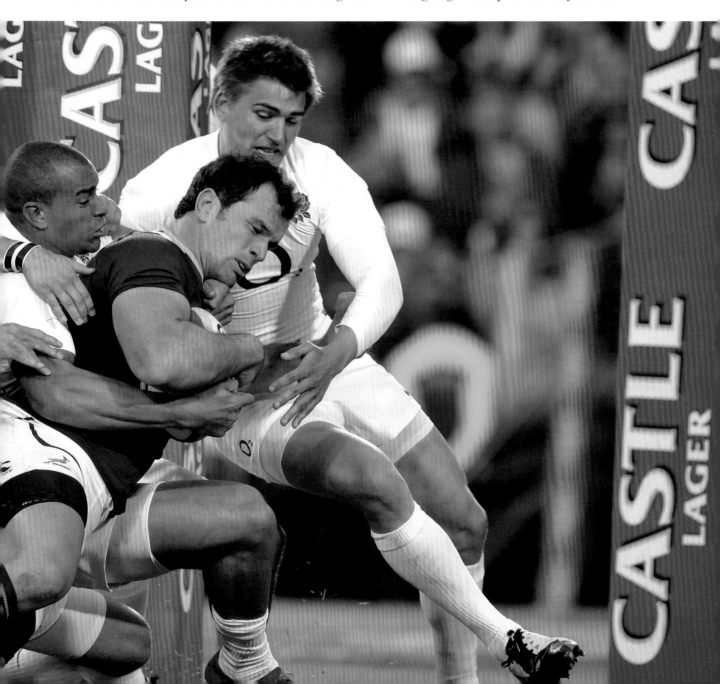

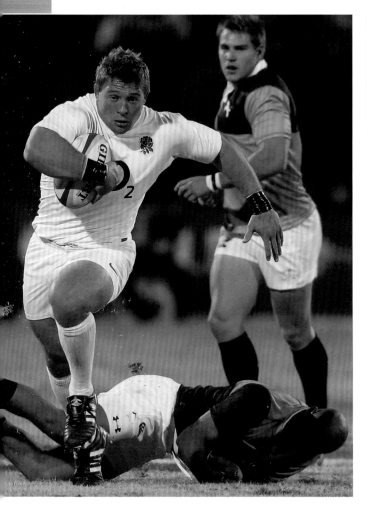

No. 9 shirt with Ben Youngs, who was already back home in England and under the surgeon's knife for a shoulder injury picked up in the second Test.

England, then, came to a satisfying final stopping-off point. The Test series was, self-evidently, the centrepiece of the tour. It revealed weaknesses in certain players such as No. 8 Ben Morgan, whose conditioning needed a certain uplift; wing David Strettle, too, perhaps, who has lost a half-yard of pace when set against the very best. But there was more benefit to be gained than just a 14-point differential over a three-Test series, a slender deficit that spoke of an England team that had soul and togetherness.

Lancaster had also insisted on two midweek matches, against two Barbarians combinations, in Kimberley and Potchefstroom. The games were invaluable for England as they looked to sift through the next tier of players to see who might be able to step up another level.

England were flaky and inconsistent in the first midweek game. They rattled up a 25-7 lead by midway through the first half, tries coming from No. 8 Thomas Waldrom, Wasps flyer Christian Wade and Quins centre George Lowe, and looked as if they were about to romp to victory. Instead, they showed a soft underbelly, allowed the Barbarians to come back at them and were grateful in the end to be able to stretch clear to a 54-26 final scoreline, Wade bringing matters to a close with his hat-trick try.

Care's performance that day was to earn his promotion eventually to the Test starting slot: sharp, cool-headed, decisive, the Harlequin looked back to his best. Waldrom, too, came through strongly, while Wade finished well but looked vulnerable in defence.

The second midweek game also yielded some riches as well as a 57-31 win against what was a stronger Barbarians line-up drawn mainly from the Pumas. Bath full back Nick Abendanon scored a hat-trick, but the eye was really drawn to the performances of hooker Tom Youngs and Gloucester full back/wing Jonny May, who had only arrived in the country a few days earlier. May has real gas and it showed as he scored two tries in quick succession after coming on as a replacement for Harlequins wing Ugo Monye, who was knocked cold in a follow-up tackle on Barbarians scrum half Shaun Venter.

Youngs, brother of Ben, had only had a handful of starts for the Tigers after being encouraged to switch position from centre to hooker by Springbok coach Meyer, who had had a seven-month coaching stint at Leicester four years earlier. Youngs is a tough yet athletic player, the sort of ball-carrying front-row forward that England need. His line-out throwing needs to become more consistent, but this tour certainly enhanced his prospects.

There were others who advanced their cause, too. Quins full back Mike Brown showed well in the first Test, elevated over Ben Foden who was switched to wing, as indeed he was in the final Test to accommodate Alex Goode of Saracens. Brown injured a thumb and was ruled out of the rest of the tour. Goode, though, was one of the success stories of the third Test. Foden has a real fight on his hands for the No. 15 shirt. Exeter Chiefs flanker Tom Johnson, meanwhile, featured in all three internationals, showing his energy in that opening Test, understandable naivety at times, too.

Two quick tries in succession from Morné Steyn and Jean de Villiers early in the second half sealed the first Test in Durban, England getting consolation on the scoreboard with a try from Foden in the last sequence of the game. The second Test was stark and brutal, a brooding Ellis Park the perfect backdrop for such an exhibition of raw power. England had given a debut to 21-year-old outside centre Jonathan Joseph, and while he was not exposed, he was barely able to lay hands on ball as the Springboks cut loose with tries from the irrepressible Willem Alberts, the equally indomitable Bismarck du Plessis and scrum half Francois Hougaard. England were staring at the sort of disaster that was to befall Ireland, but they rallied, captain Chris Robshaw leading from the front. Toby Flood scored a first-half try after a smart tap penalty from Ben Youngs, with the scrum half himself scoring two after the interval, both from short range. England had closed to within four points at 31-27 in the last quarter, only for a late try from JP Pietersen to extend the margin to a more deserving nine points.

England made a raft of changes for the final Test, handing full debuts to Goode and Waldrom. Robshaw had been ruled out with a hand injury, the captaincy passing to Dylan Hartley. There was far more bite and devil to England's play, an approach that might have had better return if Flood had not been injured early in the match. Care celebrated his return with a typically opportunist try in the 11th minute, Pietersen replying in the second half. The 14-14 scoreline was about right on the night.

This had to be a springboard moment for England, a result that lifted them back to fourth in the IRB rankings. They were in good heart as they headed home, and rightly so.

Plug into
our network

NEXUS

www.nexusgroup.co.uk

Scotland Down Under

by ALAN LORIMER

'In the event the game against Australia became one of personal survival, as high winds, torrential rain and low temperatures wiped out all chances of playing running rugby'

If Scottish rugby had been at a low ebb at the end of the 2012 Six Nations Championship, then three months on from its nasty nadir there was to be a transformational shift in fortune. Scotland, after suffering a whitewash in the northern hemisphere's showcase competition, embarked on a summer tour to the southern hemisphere and returned triumphant with a 100 per cent record, proving to themselves and others they were not the incompetents their Six Nations performances had suggested.

Of course planning for a successful summer tour means choosing your opposition carefully. In opting to play Tests against Fiji and Samoa, Scotland were, at a stroke, recognising their own lower international ranking while simultaneously satisfying the wishes of the IRB that touring sides should play Tests in the Pacific Island countries.

Into the mix then came Australia. The Wallabies' main focus was a Test series against the Six Nations champions, Wales, but they had agreed to play Scotland in a build-up match. By arranging

a Test match against the Scots on a Tuesday, just days before the first game against Wales, it was clear that Australia were treating the Scots less than reverentially.

Moreover, the Scotland game was scheduled to be played at Newcastle in New South Wales, not one of the recognised Test venues. Australia, too, had announced a team containing five new caps – a sixth was to earn national honours off the bench. But surely a Wallaby team even at less than full strength would be good enough to see off the Six Nations whipping boys.

Scotland came into the Test at Hunter Stadium in Newcastle on the back of seven straight defeats and intent on addressing what was a chronic lack of tries. Scott Johnson, the Australian former coach of Wales, USA and the Ospreys, had replaced Gregor Townsend as the attack coach, and the hope was that against an Australia side expected to play ball-in-the-hand rugby, Scotland would catch the bug.

Sadly for both teams the weather intervened. What had started as a sunny Tuesday in Newcastle morphed into the city's darkest night as the mother of all storms swept in from the Tasman. In the event the game became one of personal survival, as high winds, torrential rain and low temperatures wiped out all chances of playing running rugby, turning the match into a dour battle between the forward packs.

In which context Scotland emerged the better, their front row being the stronger in the tight and their back row the more aggressive round the fringes. But in spite of drives at the line, darts round the side of the scrum and the very occasional use of the backs, it all came down to kicks. Into stoppage time the scores were level at 6-6, when Australia not for the first time revealed their perennial frailities in the front row. Down went the Wallaby scrum and up went the referee's arm, leaving Scotland's diminutive fly half, Greig Laidlaw, to kick his third penalty for a shock 9-6 victory.

If Scotland were able to achieve success in conditions more akin to a December day in Glasgow, then how would they fare in the heat and humidity of Fiji? The Scots gave themselves over a week to acclimatise, a decision that proved to be a key factor in achieving victory over the unpredictable Fijians. Another factor which was to be hugely important for the Scots was the entry onto the international stage of the Edinburgh winger Tim Visser. The '*fliegende Holländer*', different to that which Wagner had envisaged, had waited three years to earn the residential qualification to play for Scotland and on 12 June 2012 that right was his.

Visser was the top try scorer in the RaboDirect PRO12 league and was the kind of strike runner that Scotland needed to address their lack of touchdowns. In the event the big Dutchman fully justified the hype surrounding his selection with two tries, one at the end of each half, as Scotland held off a late challenge by the Fijians to win 37-25 in the drainingly humid conditions of Churchill Park in Lautoka. Twenty-two of the Scotland points were scored by Laidlaw – a try, four conversions and three penalties – the visitors' other score being a penalty try. Fiji, however, tested the tourists to the core with some brilliant attacking rugby that brought them back from a 27-11 position to within two points of the Scots, only for Laidlaw and Visser to restore stability to the listing ship with ten points between them.

If Fiji was enervatingly hot for rugby, then Samoa was off the scale. Scotland had last visited Apia in 1993, when in temperatures of 95 degrees and with a similar humidity figure, the Scots wilted long before half-time.

Samoa came into the Test against Scotland as Pacific Nations Cup winners with three straight victories under their belt, and on their own turf they reckoned Scotland were beatable. It seemed they were right after fly half Tusi Pisi scored a dropped goal, two penalties, a try and a conversion to give Samoa a 16-10 lead; Scotland had accumulated their points from a try by Joe Ansbro and a penalty and conversion from Laidlaw.

Andy Robinson then brought Mike Blair on for Chris Cusiter, and the Edinburgh scrum half quickly influenced the outcome from a quick tap penalty that ended with new cap Rob Harley plunging over for a try. Laidlaw's conversion provided the winning points.

And that was it. The 2012 squad had become the first Scotland team to return from a southern-hemisphere tour unbeaten. More importantly the tour restored a measure of confidence to the Scotland coach, Andy Robinson, and to his squad of players. Robinson had felt the chill wind of criticism after the Six Nations run of defeats, and the inevitable sack-the-coach whispers, but after the summer tour, faith in the former Bath man returned.

The tour also brought more players into the competitive pool for international places, among them loose-head props Ryan Grant and Jon Welsh. Others included lock Tom Ryder and back-row Harley. It also confirmed the quality of flanker Alasdair Strokosch, who was perhaps the pick of the forwards, and fellow back-row Ross Rennie.

BELOW Matt Scott, who started at inside centre in all three Tests, runs into Lolo Lui (22) and comrade against Samoa at Apia Park.

Behind the scrum, Visser was the talk of the town, but moving up the rankings is inside centre Matt Scott. Nick De Luca after a poor Six Nations rediscovered his form, while top scorer Laidlaw was the supreme orchestra maestro, the former Jed-Forest half back exuding an assuring composure throughout to make sure Scotland's South Sea bubble never burst.

Wales in Australia

by GRAHAM CLUTTON

'Wales were certainly capable. Playing a high-tempo, high-intensity game, they were as well equipped as any touring Wales side since the heady days of the 1970s'

'Close, but no cigar' would be the most appropriate way of summing up the Wales tour to Australia in June. Three close calls for the Six Nations Grand Slam champions, but sadly three more defeats at the hands of their hosts. It's now 11 games and 33 years since the national team beat the Wallabies on Australian soil.

However, despite another tour whitewash, Wales can take heart from three defiant displays that might, on three different days, have brought greater reward. Little wonder, therefore, that caretaker coach Rob Howley was full of praise for the manner in which his side performed. Disappointment, of course, but there was clear evidence of continued progress.

'I thought the group of players were outstanding,' said Howley, who took over in charge for the tour after Warren Gatland suffered serious heel injuries in a fall at Easter at his New Zealand home.

'It was 3-0, it was a whitewash and we're not hiding away from that. However, there was a great deal in terms of ingredients. I think the players can be very proud of their efforts.'

One or two individual and very costly errors apart, they certainly can. What's more, it was a far cry from the desperate days of the 1990s when Wales shipped 40 points or more on three separate occasions against their hosts.

'We have left a marker in Australia which we're quite proud of,' added Howley, whose job had been made a little easier at the outset when Scarlets pair Scott Williams and Jonathan Davies, plus captain Sam Warburton, who had missed the final two months of the domestic season through injury, made the long haul Down Under.

Despite the absence of Jamie Roberts and injuries in the first Test to Toby Faletau, Williams and George North, Howley felt that a series win was well within the squad's capability. 'We definitely felt capable of winning,' said Howley. 'We didn't go down there with any intention of losing. We felt in good shape and the guys were keen to rewrite the history books. It just didn't work out that way.'

Wales were certainly capable, just as they had been throughout the Six Nations. Playing a high-tempo, high-intensity game, they were as well equipped as any touring Wales side since the heady days of the 1970s. There was strength in depth and a collective will to bring to an end that unwanted record of not having beaten Australia in their own backyard since the summer of '69. It was therefore hugely disappointing in the first Test, in Brisbane, when Australia led 10-0 and 17-3. However, in the face of adversity, Wales were defiant if nothing else. They cut the deficit and at one stage trailed 20-19 courtesy of an Alex Cuthbert try and 14 points from the boot of Leigh Halfpenny. The Cardiff Blues full back was far and away the stand-out performer on the tour and his accuracy with the boot was unerring. In the end, however, Pat McCabe rushed in for a try and the Wallabies won 27-19.

Howley said, 'We scored a great try and created opportunities for two more, but international rugby is about mastering those moments. International rugby is about taking those chances when they arrive. That was the difference. Australia were clinical and showed their skills under pressure.

'Looking back, it was a golden opportunity spurned. Still, we understand that it's about learning, so as long as we take the lesson on board, I'm happy. We certainly showed the watching world that we can put Australia under pressure.'

If the first Test was disappointing, the second, in Melbourne, was nothing short of heartbreaking. This time Wales led from the second minute, thanks to a try from North and a Halfpenny conversion. They were 13-7 down at the interval but led on four separate occasions in the second half before a penalty from Mike Harris, with the final kick of the game, denied Howley a victory that would have been thoroughly deserved. Sadly, it was the side's inability to control the game in the closing moments that was to prove so costly as Australia won 25-23.

'We were quite clinical when we had the ball and took our opportunities, but we just gave them one too many opportunities to get that kick at goal with indiscipline in certain areas,' he said.

'I said to the guys they could take great heart from their performance because we defended well, especially in the first half. We got off our line very quickly and made our tackles. In the second half, it was through our defence that we scored our try. But in the final couple of minutes we made a couple of wrong decisions and it cost us the game.

'We'll be better for that but it was hard to swallow at the time. In international rugby there's a fine margin between winning and losing.'

It could, and perhaps should, have been third time lucky. Unfortunately, it was anything but. Australia led the final Test in Sydney 12-9 at half-time before a try from Ryan Jones, converted by Halfpenny, edged Wales in front 16-12. The Wallabies hit back, and though Halfpenny's 70th-minute penalty put Wales within touching distance, Berrick Barnes converted a penalty five minutes from the end to seal a 3-0 whitewash 20-19.

'I think I played in many Welsh teams that got so close and yet so far,' said Howley.

'This Welsh team wants to win international games and we've come very close on three occasions. But as I said at the outset, the one thing you need to do to gain respect is to win in Australia, Sadly, we've come up short.'

Of course, three defeats in as many games brought with it criticism and question marks over Howley's suitability to the role. The simple fact is that Wales are seen as a genuine force within the world game. The fact that defeat on Australian soil is regarded as something of a missed opportunity details exactly how far this side has travelled since the depths of despair at the World Cup in 2007.

Yes, Martyn Williams and namesake Shane have chosen to hang up their international boots, but there is a rich seam of talent inside the Welsh game, and players like North, Justin Tipuric, Cuthbert, Dan Lydiate, Faletau and Lloyd Williams are still young men, who have yet to achieve their outstanding potential.

'I think the game is in decent shape and though we were beaten, I thought there was enough in our performances to show that we are developing well as a nation,' said Howley.

Wales will get an immediate shot at the Wallabies when the sides lock horns as part of the autumn series in Cardiff. As for Howley's own position, the tour will certainly have given him an indication of what could lie ahead should the Welsh Rugby Union choose to appoint the former Wales scrum half as Gatland's successor after the 2015 World Cup.

BELOW Ryan Jones crashes over in Sydney. Leigh Halfpenny converted to put Wales 16-12 in the lead with a quarter of the third Test remaining.

'I thoroughly enjoyed the opportunity and the challenge that the tour presented.

'It was challenging, but I had fantastic support from my fellow coaches. Warren has got a lot to be thanked for, because he has given us our head on several occasions over the last three or four years.'

Ireland in New Zealand

by PETER O'REILLY

'Coach Declan Kidney tried to put a brave face on it. He stressed the value of having such concentrated contact with the best rugby team in the world'

This was billed as an historic tour, the first time Ireland would ever play a three-Test series in New Zealand, and historic it proved to be – for all the wrong reasons. For this was the tour during which Ireland suffered their heaviest ever defeat, a 60-0 drubbing that was painful to witness, and hugely embarrassing for the tourists. No matter that the previous week in Christchurch they had come within a dodgy refereeing decision of beating the world champions and creating history of a different kind. Unfortunately, the tour will be remembered first and foremost for the 'Hamilton Hammer Horror'.

Right from the first time it appeared on the schedule, the wisdom of this expedition looked questionable. For sure, you could understand the reasoning of the SANZAR nations, who argued that it was very difficult for them to sell one-off Tests against European opposition, acting merely as warm-ups for the main event of their winter – the Tri-Nations, or as it has become, the Rugby Championship. A three-Test series, they argued, introduced a competitive element that would draw bigger crowds. Yet we always wondered how competitive Ireland would be in the month of June, at the end of a busy season. And this happened to be the busiest season on record. Because of the World Cup, Ireland had already played 14 Tests before they even arrived in New Zealand. The very fact that they were travelling to New Zealand for the second time in eight months only seemed to add to the sense of fatigue.

The venture was particularly tough on the Leinster contingent, whose last couple of weeks' preparation included not one cup final but two. Having beaten Ulster in the Heineken Cup final on the second-last Saturday in May, they were pipped by the Ospreys in the RaboDirect PRO12 decider at the RDS. Watching the Ospreys going up to collect their medals, some of the Leinster players looked physically and emotionally shattered. Not the best way to be feeling before a long-haul flight into a New Zealand winter.

ABOVE Julian Savea is about to touch down for one of his three tries on debut in Auckland.

FACING PAGE A try by Conor Murray helped Ireland build a 10-0 lead in the second Test, but the All Blacks stole the match at the last ditch.

PAGE 69 Scrum time in Christchurch. Ireland travelled south with a number of key forwards missing.

Coach Declan Kidney tried to put a brave face on it. He stressed the value of having such concentrated contact with the best rugby team in the world. 'I just wish we had a fourth Test against them,' he chirped at a farewell press conference. This was maybe testing credibility.

It was hard to travel with any genuine hope, especially with such a lightweight pack. Paul O'Connell's absence through injury meant that Ulster's Dan Tuohy would be making his first Test start. Peter O'Mahony, a flanker in his first international season, would stand in for Stephen Ferris. Mike Ross's hamstring injury meant that Ulster's Declan Fitzpatrick was in line to make his Test debut opposite grizzled veteran Tony Woodcock. This was a scary prospect.

So much for the received wisdom about the tourists' best chance on summer tours coming in the first Test. New Zealand hadn't played together since the World Cup final in October, but it still turned into a sort of belated lap of honour for the returning heroes, who won 42-10 against disappointingly flat opponents. It was a special evening for one new All Black, winger Julian Savea, winner of the IRB's Young Player of the Year in 2010 and someone who was already having to deal with comparisons with Jonah Lomu. As it turned out, Savea didn't disappoint, scoring a hat-trick of tries on his Test debut.

Most dispiriting of all for Kidney was that two of Savea's tries were 'run-ins' – touchdowns where not a finger was laid on him by an opponent. We knew Ireland might struggle in the set-pieces but at least expected a frenzied intensity in defence, inspired by fear as much as anything else. But they allowed the Kiwis far too much time on the ball and paid a heavy price. Fergus McFadden's solitary second-half try was no real consolation, as the All Blacks had run in five tries of their own.

So things were looking grim, with the home team now making an emotional return to Christchurch, a city they had not graced since the earthquake of September 2010 – the game was to be played at Rugby League Park in the suburb of Addington, as AMI Stadium was awaiting reconstruction. Maybe newly installed All Blacks coach Steve Hansen believed that merely being in Christchurch would draw another big performance from his side; instead they scraped home, with Hansen being gracious enough to admit afterwards that Ireland had been robbed.

The key difference for the tourists was that they built an early 10-0 lead, based on Conor Murray's sniping try, which showed that the All Blacks can look a different side when they are rattled. Even Dan Carter and Richie McCaw made basic errors. Ireland, meanwhile, played with a controlled fury that saw them turn around still in front at 10-9.

At 19-19 in the 70th minute, and with Israel Dagg in the sin-bin, you were backing Ireland, until a few critical things went against them. First, Jonny Sexton missed a longish penalty; second, referee Nigel Owens penalised them at the scrum, a phase in which they had dominated; and third, an errant Carter dropped-goal attempt clipped an Irish finger on its way over the dead-ball line, thus affording the Kiwis another attacking scrum. Carter didn't miss a second time. The tourists barely had the energy or the heart to criticise Owens afterwards. They knew they had missed a golden opportunity, and they knew there would be reprisals.

So it proved. Kidney had arranged a four-day stopover in touristy Queenstown for the first part of the final week on tour, a gesture aimed at trying to keep his players fresh, but which also sent out the message that the holidays were coming. Paddy Wallace was coming too – all the way from his holidays in Portugal, to replace the injured Gordon D'Arcy. As it turned out, Wallace wasn't 100 per cent fit himself, and it showed. Not Kidney's most inspired selection ever.

Meanwhile the All Blacks were angry. Your correspondent just happened to be staying in the same hotel as them that week, and could sense a focus and a determination to put things right.

The details of the demolition barely require repetition. But here they are anyway. New Zealand scored nine tries, including two for the irrepressible Sonny Bill Williams and two by Sam Cane, their highly promising flanker. And in response? Zilch – for the first time since Ireland's second string were beaten 16-0 by Argentina in Buenos Aires in 2007.

'As the final whistle is blown, seeing that zero against your country's name is a sick enough feeling,' said Rob Kearney afterwards. Consolations? A few rookies had their eyes opened to the realities of top-class rugby. There was that heroic defeat in Christchurch. But the main consolation is that Ireland won't tour New Zealand again until 2024.

Can we kick it?

Drop in and find out
LV.com

If you love it, L♥= it

INSURANCE ♥ INVESTMENTS ♥ RETIREMENT

HOME FRONT

Back from the Brink
Wasps under New Ownership
by CHRIS JONES

'Patently, something dramatic had to happen to save the club, and that is where former Wasps back-row forward Ken Moss has come into the equation'

When Steve Hayes, then managing director of Wycombe Wanderers FC, added ownership of London Wasps to his portfolio, it was supposed to herald a new era for the club that had ruled Europe after becoming the best team in England. Instead, under Hayes, Wasps struggled from 2008 to match their previous achievements and started to lose fans at a stadium that could not be developed due to obvious restrictions – it was in the middle of a valley on an industrial site.

Last season the former champions were staring relegation from the Premiership square in the face and had serious financial worries to surmount to ensure they remained a viable concern. It was a dramatic fall from grace for a club that under previous owner Chris Wright had won 11 trophies in 11 seasons and had set up home at Adams Park in 2002.

Patently, something dramatic had to happen to save the club, and that is where former Wasps back-row forward Ken Moss has come into the equation, heading a consortium that has kept one of the strongest brands in rugby alive by paying off the debts that had taken it to the brink of oblivion.

Heading into the new season, Moss is adamant that his fellow investors have secured the future of the club and that Wasps under director of rugby Dai Young – who endured so many headaches on and off the pitch last season – can make the headlines for the right reasons in 2012-13. The return of James Haskell and Tom Palmer is hugely encouraging, and along with the recruitment of key men such as Lions No. 10 Stephen Jones and Italy's Andrea Masi, one of the best Six Nations performers in recent years, will help convince worried Wasps fans that they can start competing at the right end of the table after having to endure the Premiership success of arch-rivals Saracens and Harlequins.

Moss knows he must win back disaffected fans to help the club coffers and said, 'Clearly the club has seen a drop in numbers at Adams Park over the past couple of years and we need to turn that around.

'Our overall aim is to get Wasps back on a sound financial footing and ensure the club is sustainable long term. We will do our bit to offer a much better match-day experience for supporters at Adams Park on and off the pitch, and in turn we need all Wasps supporters to do their bit and get down to the ground as often as they can.'

ABOVE Among the headaches for Dai Young was a string of injuries to first-teamers, including Ross Filipo (left) and club captain John Hart (right), who was forced into retirement.

FACING PAGE After spells in France with Stade Français, in Japan with the Ricoh Black Rams and in Super Rugby with the Highlanders, James Haskell (seen here during Super Rugby 2012) returns to Wasps colours for 2012-13.

Long term, Moss is looking to develop a new stadium for Wasps. Meanwhile, in the short term he wants to attract new sponsors to help their financial situation, and the club will continue to play at Adams Park. He said, 'We have come into this late but we are working extremely hard to get these in place for the start of the season. They will provide us with key investment but I must be clear that the consortium taking on ownership of the club are not doing so for emotional reasons. We are doing this for business reasons with our ambition being to stabilise the club's finances and go forward from there.

'We have a strong handle on the costs of running the business but we need to stabilise the variables such as the match-day attendances. These have got to improve and we cannot do it without the fans.'

Moss joined Wasps from Liverpool St Helens in 1985, becoming a crowd favourite with his fearless play at blind-side flanker, and after quitting rugby in 1990 – the year Wasps won the Courage League title – made his millions in IT, selling the Bytech company for 'several million'. After the sale to Avnet Computer Inc, the world's largest computer distributor, he stayed on until 2001 as European president, and in 2008 founded vzaar, one of the most successful online video platforms in the USA and Europe, boasting film director Oliver Stone as a major investor.

Chris Wright, whose financial backing helped London Wasps win those 11 trophies in 11 years, left Wasps in 2008, handing control of the club to Hayes, who last season decided to offload the former European champions after failing to gain planning permission to develop an aerodrome site in Wycombe to secure the club's future. Former owner Wright wanted to relocate Wasps to Oxford United's Kassam Stadium, but Hayes pushed for Adams Park – home of Wycombe Wanderers. Wright is adamant he would have remained at Wasps as a financial backer alongside fellow investor John O'Connell, but Hayes wanted to run the club himself in 2008. Now it is newly promoted London Welsh who are going to play at the Kassam Stadium, with Wasps as their visitors!

Wright said, 'We won the Heineken Cup the year before I left and I didn't really want to go but Steve Hayes wanted to run it himself. He was interested in running the whole shooting match rather than work with John and myself and in hindsight, I don't know why he took that decision because it could have been three of us sharing the load.

'If the load was too heavy why didn't he stick with the three of us? He felt he could do a lot better on his own.

'We did fall out over specific things including putting Lawrence [Dallaglio] on the board as soon as he retired and I felt it was unfair for Ian McGeechan, the director of rugby, to have any player on the board who he would be reporting to.

'There was also a perception – I believe – that I was happy to stay at Adams Park and wasn't looking at other options. In fact, I had spent two or three years dealing with Wycombe Council and together with Barry Hearn, who owned Orient, we spoke to the Olympic Stadium about the possibility of playing there. We even looked at playing at The Oval.

'When we first left Loftus Road, we did look at Oxford United's stadium but Steve was committed to having Wasps and Wycombe together and had this idea of using the aerodrome to build a new stadium. I thought it was a non-runner and that it would never get off the ground and I believed we had to do something else and going to Oxford was the obvious answer because of the 12,500 capacity it would give us. However, that did not suit Steve's agenda.'

Back on the pitch, Young, the director of rugby, is desperately hoping he will not have to deal with another such season. Ten first-team regulars suffered long-term problems, while Simon Shaw moved to Toulon and fellow 2003 England World Cup winners Joe Worsley and Steve Thompson retired due to injury, the fate also suffered by No. 8 Dan Ward-Smith.

The arrival of new owners will allow Young to bolster a squad that will be boosted by the return of Palmer and Haskell along with the arrival of Wales hooker Rhys Thomas. Wasps have been operating below the £4.2-million salary cap for all Premiership teams due to self-imposed funding restrictions which would be relaxed with the arrival of new money. For those long-suffering Wasps fans, the sight of 31-year-old Andrea Masi, who has been capped 69 times by Italy, will, they hope, signal the return of the good times.

"Wishing the Wooden Spoon every success with their ongoing work"

INSPIRING COMMUNITIES
CHANGING LIVES

The Saracens Sport Foundation aims to inspire communities and change lives through the power of sport. Through the Saracens brand, professional players and high quality staff, we engage and challenge children and young people to lead an active, healthy and rewarding lifestyle.

To find out more about the work of the Saracens Sport Foundation and how you can support our work, visit www.saracens.com/foundation

SARACENS
SPORT
FOUNDATION

Full House at Wembley
Saracens v Harlequins

by SARA ORCHARD

'Harlequins and Saracens sat first and second in the Aviva Premiership table, and many rugby writers had already dubbed the match a rehearsal for the final'

R ugby union in England reached new heights on 31 March 2012, when 83,761 fans packed into Wembley Stadium to watch Saracens against Harlequins in the Aviva Premiership. The bumper crowd was a new club rugby attendance record, beating by over 1500 the previous mark, set at the Leinster against Munster Heineken Cup semi-final at Dublin's Croke Park in 2009. It was also the second time the Aviva Premiership attendance record had been broken that season. Harlequins had welcomed 82,000 fans to Twickenham for the reverse fixture with Saracens in December 2011. A total of 165,761

ABOVE Wembley Stadium, 31 March 2012. The scoreboard announces that the fixture, Saracens' eighth at the home of English football, has attracted a record attendance for a club rugby match.

fans watched the two sides clash in 2011-12. These impressive figures are a credit to the hard work of the two Premiership clubs, as they continue to build the popularity of rugby union in England.

The venue for this second titanic tussle of the season is better known as the home of English football. Nevertheless, it is no stranger to rugby fans, since the old Wembley Stadium hosted 76,000 for the 1999 Five Nations clash between Wales and England, and this latest match was actually Saracens' eighth in the new arena. Their first fixture here was against Northampton Saints in September 2009 in front of 44,832, and over three years the matches and entertainment have just got bigger and better. The Wembley day out was far more than just a game of rugby union, with the north London club laying on a barnstorming pre-match show.

With the crowd beginning to flood through the Wembley turnstiles, at 2pm the entertainment began. First up was a chance for the club's grass roots to share in the big game experience, with 1000 youngsters from Saracens' partner schools and clubs forming the 'Pride in Unity' parade.

At pitchside the crowd were treated to a demonstration from another rugby side keen to display their talents. The Great Britain Wheelchair Rugby team had a huge year ahead of them with the 2012 Paralympics to be held in London in August/September. After finishing fourth at the last two Paralympic Games, Great Britain were eager to show their skills and build their support base.

Then Wembley found its groove as the Rock Choir took centre stage. A musical phenomenon sweeping across the UK, the choir has over 16,000 members and they sing everything from pop, Motown and gospel to the latest chart hits. Signed to Universal Records with a four-album deal, they have featured in their own documentary (ITV's 'The Choir That Rocks') and have made television appearances on 'The One Show', 'This Morning' and 'BBC Breakfast'. Also dubbed 'The People's Choir', they were represented by 1500 singers from Hertfordshire, Bedfordshire and Buckinghamshire, who took to the pitch to rock Wembley. Opening with Robbie Williams' 'Let Me Entertain You', the choir lived up to their billing, getting the whole of Wembley on their feet and dancing.

Saracens have built a reputation for attracting the most popular music talent to their Wembley extravaganzas. Following in the footsteps of The Saturdays, Chipmunk and Tinie Tempah, chart-toppers McFly wowed the crowd. Dougie Poynter, 2011 winner of ITV's 'I'm A Celebrity ...', and the

BBC's 'Strictly Come Dancing' winner Harry Judd were joined by band-mates Tom Fletcher and Danny Jones to play their greatest hits in the centre of the Wembley pitch. The set list included their Top Ten hits, 'All About You', '5 Colours in Her Hair' and 'Shine a Light'.

All of this, and the rugby hadn't even started. Ahead of kick-off, the match ball was to make a dramatic arrival at Wembley. The Saracens mascot, 'Sarrie' the camel, had already made a number of daredevil entrances onto the sacred turf, including flying in on a zip wire and abseiling from the roof. This time, to the accompaniment of 'Wild Thing', Sarrie and the ball arrived on top of a motorcycle display team pyramid.

Finally it was time for the rugby. Harlequins and Saracens sat first and second in the Aviva Premiership table with just three points separating them, meaning that the winner of the clash would top the table at the final whistle. Many rugby writers had already dubbed the match a rehearsal for the Aviva Premiership final, although in the event Leicester were to prove too much for Saracens in the semi-final at Welford Road.

Quins started brightly when centre Jordan Turner-Hall crossed for the first try of the game after three minutes. After Saracens and England fly half Owen Farrell reduced the deficit and then put Sarries ahead with the boot, the visitors powered to a second try through George Lowe and a third from Danny Care. Sarries' Wembley party began to look in danger as they trailed 24-12, but they hit back through scrum half Richard Wigglesworth, who burrowed over the try line in his first match back since having knee surgery in October.

Despite the conversion, the scoreline was stuck at 24-19 in favour of Quins. Saracens threw every move in their playbook at their London rivals but couldn't convert a plethora of possession into points. Quins finished the match with just 13 men as Nick Easter and Danny Care were sent to the sin-bin, but the job was done. At the final whistle, Quins had held on to their lead and the victory gave them a six-point breathing space at the top of the Aviva Premiership table.

FACING PAGE McFly were the latest big musical act laid on by Saracens for a Wembley extravaganza.

BELOW George Lowe's intervention deprives Saracens' Chris Wyles of a try.

Hail to the Chiefs
Exeter at Europe's Top Table

by STEVE BALE

'Exeter won still more friends by forswearing the attritional style with which they had come to be associated and running in to the end of last season in a blaze of attacking rugby'

Exeter have the Premiership's coach of the year in Rob Baxter, and quite right too. For some reason some folk choose to treat the Chiefs as country bumpkins, but Baxter brings a rare sophistication to what in reality is a big-city club. Which is to say 'big' by rugby standards. Exeter is not 'darkest Devon' but the self-proclaimed capital of the West Country with a rugby plan meticulously drawn up and executed by their own Devonian coach.

Under Baxter, Exeter have repeatedly exceeded the expectations of those outside Sandy Park and even, if they are really honest, occasionally their own. When they were promoted in 2010, Baxter himself understood the wide feeling that immediate relegation already threatened. In the event, the nay-sayers were rebuked by Exeter's finish in eighth place. Baxter then said that, what with the need to overcome second-season syndrome, if his side did as well in 2011-12 it would be a still greater achievement.

'A mark of our success next season would actually be to equal where we are now, because everyone knows all about us,' he declared at the time. He was too modest. The Chiefs rose to fifth and qualified for the Heineken Cup. They even had a shot at a top-four play-off place until the last

day of the regular season. Every performance indicator measured another major improvement from the one made in the year after they were Championship champions.

'There's no secret. We've told plenty of people about it,' said Baxter. 'We sat down with the players pre-season and, simple as it sounds, our only aim was to be a bit better than the previous year, whether that was in points gained or place in the league table.

'Either way, we would have taken it as a success. Other than get better in lots of areas, we didn't set too many goals. It didn't include getting into Europe but it certainly did include getting out of our Amlin Challenge Cup pool.'

So it came to pass. Exeter went to Paris and ruefully appreciate they should have beaten Stade Français – the sort of fixture, let alone scalp, that was imaginable only as a distant dream in all those years they were seeking a Premiership place. Moreover, Exeter won still more friends by forswearing the attritional style with which they had come to be associated and running in to the end of last season in a blaze of attacking, free-spirited rugby after the aridity of a three-point home defeat by Bath in February.

'The turning point was losing that game at Sandy Park,' said Baxter. 'We hadn't done anything. We'd felt our way through a game, thought we could squeeze out a victory. Mentally we got it all wrong, but we decided there and then we were going to go after games. It fired us up.'

The fired-up Baxter has a neat line about statistics: 'There's not one stat other than the scoreboard that tells you who wins.' But he is mildly disingenuous because other figures, as laid out in the Premiership's finishing table, do tell a tale of Exeter's solid development. In 2010-11, the promoted team won 10 and lost 12, achieved five losing bonus points and none for try-scoring. So they took something from 15 of their 22 fixtures, itself a fine post-promotion achievement. They were 20 points clear of relegated Leeds.

Last season Exeter won 12 and lost 10, were 27 ahead of bottom-placed Newcastle and gained three try-scoring bonuses and eight for losing by seven points or fewer. So only twice in the entire season – at

FACING PAGE Chiefs head coach and Premiership coach of the year Rob Baxter gets a vote of confidence on match day at Sandy Park.

BELOW Argentine international Gonzalo Camacho touches down for Exeter in their 18-11 win over London Irish in round 19 of the 2011-12 Premiership.

Northampton and Saracens – were they empty-handed. This statistic, equalled only by Saracens and exceeded by no one else, is more telling than Baxter perhaps might acknowledge. It shows his players have a precious indomitability and esprit de corps which augment their underappreciated ability.

'There is more to Exeter than fighting spirit, though we do have plenty of that,' said Baxter. 'We are a better rugby side, with more talented players in breadth and depth than people have sometimes given us credit for.

'We bring good attention to detail. We know individual performances turn on what the individuals themselves do, so we concentrate plenty on each individual's role in the team, one to one with the coaches.

'This ensures each player knows his worth in and to the team. Wanting to be in the Premiership is a huge motivation for a player who has been in Championship finals. But now our motivation is something different.

'We talk to our players now about whether they can get international caps. Saracens did it: they had a team who didn't have any England players. Then you win the Premiership and you get a few.'

True enough, the elevation of the best of Baxter's Chiefs to the Test arena would be a significant next step even if it were inconvenient to Baxter himself as coach. The process made a start with Tom Johnson's inclusion in England's tour party to South Africa in June. He was in the starting XV in all three Tests. This exceptional flanker had been around the second-string Saxons for more than a year so had been a contender of sorts. Scrum half Haydn Thomas' selection in a 27-man squad before England played the Barbarians in May was further recognition.

Johnson and Thomas, both 30, are prime examples of the influence Baxter can have, and has had, on late developers whose careers had more or less flatlined – Johnson's at Coventry, Thomas' at Gloucester and Bristol – until Devon's call, or in Thomas' case recall. Thomas began his career at Exeter before sampling a higher life elsewhere in the west. For Baxter, Thomas and Johnson really ought to be the harbingers of a regular and growing presence in Stuart Lancaster's England squads.

'We are an English club playing in the premier competition in the country and we should be trying to get our English players to play for England,' said Baxter. 'I would love for Exeter to produce an England international, and sooner rather than later.'

As a stalwart who followed in his father John's footsteps in the Exeter pack and has been succeeded by his own kid brother Richard, Rob Baxter knows his local sporting history. This club used to be a power in the land. But it is some 48 years since wing Adrian Underwood won the last of his five caps, longer still since club president Dick Manley was in the England back row through the 1963 Five Nations.

Some of us are, alas, senior enough to have been present when, aged 30, Manley was one of seven new caps – six in the pack – when England won at Cardiff Arms Park for the last time for 28 years. Here is his match-programme (price: one shilling) entry: 'Captain of Exeter and also captain of Devon, for whom he has played 56 times. He has played 12 times for the Barbarians and in 13 seasons with Exeter has made more than 450 appearances.

'He has played in seven England trials spread over six years, playing at open-side wing forward and No 8 and now at blind-side wing forward, the position which he occupies for England. Has played against every major touring side that has visited this country.'

In other words Dick Manley had to undergo a pre-international apprenticeship which would stretch the patience of any modern player but may actually encourage the likes of Tom Johnson. As Exeter Chiefs have repeatedly proved, no cause is ever lost.

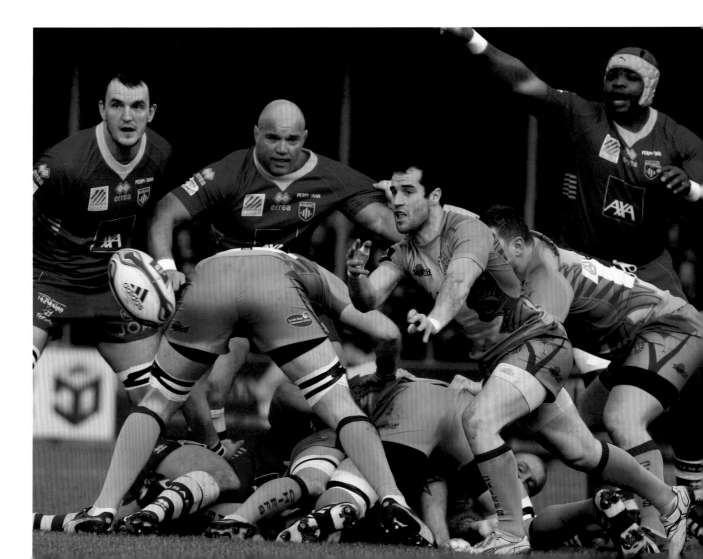

On a Roll
Michaela Staniford and England
by **SARA ORCHARD**

'England won a seventh consecutive title with another Grand Slam, but for Staniford the moment of the tournament was winning her fiftieth cap against France'

The juggernaut that is the England Women rugby team continued to gain speed and popularity in the 2011-12 season. Two years out from the 2014 Women's Rugby World Cup in France and the team have shown they are on track in their attempt to finally be crowned world champions, with phenomenal success in all areas of the game. Having met and lost to New Zealand in the last three World Cup

BELOW Michaela Staniford makes a break for England against New Zealand at Twickenham, November 2011.

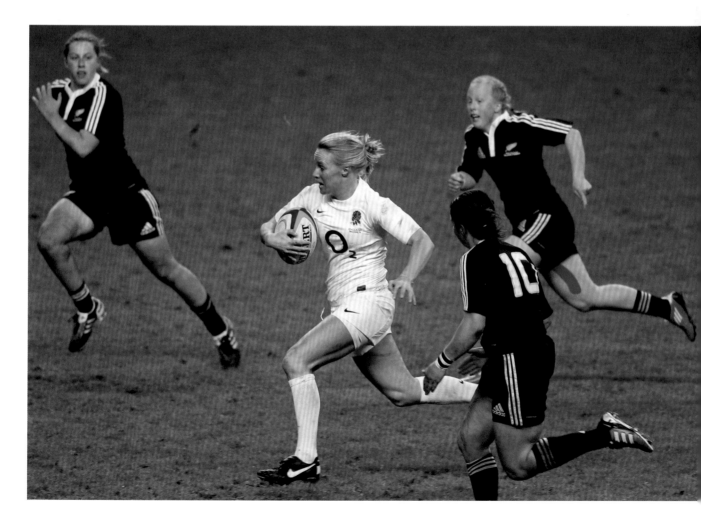

finals, England Women have put in some incredible performances in the last 12 months, with hopes that there could finally be a shift in the world order.

One player who has been involved in every step of England's domination of the women's game this season is London Wasps wing Michaela Staniford. The 25-year-old was part of the squad that beat New Zealand in the three-Test autumn series. She then helped the squad to a seventh successive RBS 6 Nations title, as well as captaining the England Women's Sevens team to IRB Women's Sevens Challenge Cup victories in Hong Kong, London, Holland and Moscow.

The Hertfordshire schoolteacher admits she's still taking it all in. 'The amount I've achieved has been massive. I haven't even had the time to look back at the magnitude of what happened to me as a player, because I don't think it will ever happen again.'

Back in November, England completed a home series win over reigning world champions New Zealand. The three-Test rubber was wrapped up after England claimed victories in the first two matches, played at Twickenham and Esher respectively. The final match in the series, also at Esher, finished in a draw. Staniford admitted it was a significant step forward for England. 'It was big for us. We started breaking down barriers against a team that has almost been untouchable and at the top of the world for a long time.

'Having the series win under our belts is showing that England players can not only do it once but we can do it repeatedly, and that was really key. Not only that but a lot of young players were involved in those Tests. I think for the future and moving on that will help take us a step closer to our goal of a World Cup winner's medal.'

After the emphatic series victory over New Zealand came the RBS 6 Nations Women's Championship in February and March. Having won the title for the previous six years (five of them Grand Slams), England Women once again went into the tournament as the team to beat. Once again Staniford was in the thick of it. 'We're very seasoned in the Six Nations now and all the other teams love playing us because we're the team to bring down, and I don't think England would have that any other way.'

England won a seventh consecutive title with another Grand Slam (indeed, no team scored a try against them), but for Staniford the moment of the tournament was winning her fiftieth cap against France in Paris. After the match the teams had a rare chance to join the England and France men's sides for their RBS 6 Nations post-match function. Staniford was presented with her fiftieth cap by RFU president Willie Wildash to a standing ovation. 'That was an experience that I was lucky enough to have, that I don't think any woman has ever had (although I hope they do have in the future). It was just so exciting being in that environment let alone being the talking point. It was something that I was very, very lucky and proud to be a part of.'

Following the Six Nations Staniford's attention turned to her role as co-captain of the England Women's Sevens team. The team's goal was to qualify for the 2013 IRB Rugby World Cup Sevens in Moscow and this was achieved following Challenge Cup wins in Hong Kong, London, Holland and Moscow.

'It's amazing when you talk about it all in one sentence. Hong Kong was a sensational experience. The crowd made it so special along with the recognition we got from some of the players that we've always just watched from a distance. Myself and Sonia Green were stood on the pitchside and had Serge Betsen walk up to us and say "Your match was fantastic, well done." I was gobsmacked, my jaw dropped to the floor for the rest of the week.

'Then we went to London and with the home crowd we wanted to be a team that England is proud of. We learned a bit more about the team, we made some changes from Hong Kong to make it a little bit more experienced. The win was key to get more people watching England Women play rugby.'

In 2016 rugby Sevens will become an Olympic sport and Michaela has noticed that the game's profile has been changing as a result. 'A few people have been dropping the whole Rio 2016 into the equation over the last few months. It's something you can't deny that you would want to be a part of. To be an Olympian is another level and is ultimately the pinnacle of any sportsperson's career and the chance to be involved in that would be massive.'

Before 2016, Michaela has plenty to keep her busy. Following England's success on the Sevens circuit, they have now qualified for the 2013 Sevens World Cup in Moscow, and Staniford hopes she'll be a part of the team. 'It's a massive aim of mine. It's a lot on the body and I would love to be involved but at the moment I think we'll just take it step by step and tournament by tournament.'

FACING PAGE Paris, 11 March 2012. Michaela Staniford leads out England on the occasion of her fiftieth cap.

BELOW Short-game success. Skipper Staniford lifts the Cup after England Women win the Sevens in Hong Kong.

DTZ is proud to support Wooden Spoon
The children's charity of rugby

www.dtz.com

Transforming the world
of property services

The Stoop Conquers
the 2011-12 Aviva Premiership
by CHRIS HEWETT

'The try count in the final finished two apiece but Quins were
the better side – and Robshaw, at the hub of everything, was
the best of Quins'

The trouble with accidents waiting to happen is that just occasionally something brings the
waiting to an end. London Welsh emerged as that something during the fag end of an
exhausting domestic campaign that had, at its outset, appeared certain to be defined by the
2011 World Cup in New Zealand rather than by events on the outskirts of Richmond, that sylvan
corner of the capital where the ghosts of great amateur players past had long seemed more tangible
than the flesh-and-blood realities of professional players present.

ABOVE No way through for Richard Haughton of Wasps against the Falcons as Newcastle beat their fellow strugglers at High Wycombe on the last day of the regular season – but not by enough.

PAGE 91 Harlequins lift the Premiership trophy for the first time after beating Leicester 30-23 in the final at Twickenham.

If no one questioned the Exiles' status as a great club of a bygone era, few registered their sudden rise as serious promotion candidates until the latter weeks of the season, by which time the Premiership's 'minimum criteria' regulations governing access to the top flight of English club rugby looked as vulnerable as a seven-stone weakling at a sumo tournament. Regulations are all well and good until someone threatens to test them in a court of law, and as London Welsh had some unusually able legal minds on their side, the criteria road-crash grew more inevitable by the day once the on-field business was finally completed in May.

So it was that after an initial rejection by the Rugby Football Union, who in truth had no desire to block promotion and even less stomach for a prolonged argument before Mr Justice Cocklecarrot, the right conclusion was reached – a little late in the day, but better late than never. Even in Newcastle, that most exposed outpost of the union game in these islands, there cannot have been many rugby followers who failed to see that by ending up at the foot of the Premiership table after bottom-third finishes in each of the previous five seasons, the Tynesiders had paid the going rate for systemic failure.

Newcastle had looked weak from the start of the season: never had the ambitious muscularity of purpose that defined them when a combination of Sir John Hall's money and Rob Andrew's ruthless approach to team-building brought the inaugural Premiership title to Kingston Park a dozen years previously seemed so distant. The only question for most observers was whether Worcester, on their return to the big league at the expense of Leeds, had the wherewithal to make sufficient sense of the 22-match programme to stay up. This was not a given, but Richard Hill and his high-powered Sixways coaching team – headed by the two Phils, Davies and Larder – knew enough to plot a route through the minefield, even without the leadership skills of the resourceful flanker Pat Sanderson, forced to give best to a chronic shoulder injury a fortnight or so before the opening round of fixtures.

As the season unfolded, Newcastle's best hope of survival turned out to be Wasps – one of the most successful outfits in club rugby history but now in freefall, thanks to a profoundly unhealthy combination of big-name retirements, debilitating injuries, managerial miscalculation and acute financial discomfort. The former champions had lured David Young across the Severn Bridge from Cardiff and installed him as director of rugby, and with rugby thinkers as intelligent as Paul Turner and Trevor Woodman among the backroom staff, not to mention the continuing effectiveness of Rob Smith's academy set-up, there was no obvious reason at the beginning of the campaign to fear for their safety. Bottom four, yes; bottom one, no. But for all the efforts of the youngsters expertly prepared by Smith – the wing Christian Wade, the centre Elliot Daly, the forwards Joe Launchbury, Sam Jones and Billy Vunipola – they were deep in the smelly stuff come the final rounds.

But for Sam Vesty's premature celebrations in the penultimate game against Bath at the Recreation Ground – the former Leicester player committed the fundamental howler of revelling in a try before he had actually managed to complete it, and was duly blindsided by the ultra-rapid Tom Varndell – the High Wycombe-based Londoners would not have taken anything from the contest and therefore would have been one straight defeat away from relegation. As their opponents in the last match were, of all people, Newcastle … well, you can imagine how fraught life would have been at Adams Park on the afternoon of Saturday 5 May. In the event, Wasps knew that they could lose narrowly and still stay up, which is precisely what they did.

At the 'all sweetness and light' end of the table, a long way from the darkness of the lower reaches, things were anything but sweetness and light. Richard Cockerill, the Leicester director of rugby and one of the more vigorously outspoken members of the union fraternity, declared at the pre-season launch that World Cup calls would make his life extremely difficult – and, perhaps, his job unsafe. Other DoRs and head coaches who would be losing significant numbers of players to England duty, like Jim Mallinder at Northampton, no doubt felt the same way.

Sure enough, both of the major East Midlands clubs struggled from the get-go: Leicester lost five of their first half-dozen games – if their home defeat by Exeter on the opening weekend was barely believable, their shipping of 50 points to Saracens in front of the Welford Road faithful was positively jaw-dropping – while their neighbours were scarcely more comfortable until the likes of Ben Foden, Chris Ashton, Dylan Hartley, Courtney Lawes and Tom Wood returned from All Black country.

Who was taking advantage of the turmoil? Step forward Exeter, who would raise eyebrows across the land by securing Heineken Cup status at only their second attempt, and Harlequins, brilliantly managed by Conor O'Shea and superbly coached by that splendid Premiership greybeard John Kingston. There had been signs the previous season that the pastel-shaded city slickers of old were gathering significant momentum and now, with a strong start behind them, they engaged a high gear and zoomed off into the distance, arriving at the top of the table before September was out and staying there for the duration.

So many Quins performed outstandingly well – the pugnacious full back Mike Brown, the resilient centre Jordan Turner-Hall, the outside-half craftsman Nick Evans, the troubled but unfailingly effervescent scrum half Danny Care, the bristling young prop Joe Marler, the increasingly influential front-rower James Johnston, the ever-willing lock George Robson – that when new England boss Stuart Lancaster showed his first selectorial hand ahead of the Six Nations, few died of shock at the size of the contingent from the Stoop. This was headed by the flanker Chris Robshaw, who fought off the perceived challenge of his back-row rival Wood to succeed Lewis Moody as national captain. If ever a man justified the faith placed in him by a red-rose coach, that man was Robshaw.

Disappointed at missing out on World Cup selection (he insisted this was the case, even though any right-minded human being would, in retrospect, have avoided the tragic-comic pantomime in New Zealand like the plague), Robshaw redoubled his efforts at club level, enjoying a golden run of victories that stretched all the way to Christmas. If there were those who, while admiring the Trojan-like industriousness of his rugby, wondered whether he might be more of a '6½' rather than a genuine breakaway specialist, even they had to confess midway through the campaign that whatever the captain was or wasn't, he was damned good.

Combining cleverly with the Samoan flanker Maurie Fa'asavalu, to educated eyes one of the stand-out loose forwards at the World Cup, and the discarded international No. 8 Nick Easter, the

Quins skipper repeatedly found ways of giving his side an edge. If the Londoners' victories in the second half of the season were less comprehensive than they had been in the first, it was at least partly because of his absence on England business. When Robshaw returned from the Six Nations, he led the club to a famous victory over Saracens in front of a record 83,761 crowd at Wembley, thereby putting the club within touching distance of a home tie in the play-offs.

It was not all plain sailing from there. Far from it. A revitalised Northampton, driven from half back by the indefatigable Lee Dickson, were a major threat on semi-final day at the Stoop, just as Saracens, resourcefully led by the much maligned (and wrongly maligned) Steve Borthwick, were equipped to ask some very awkward questions of Leicester in the other game. But Quins fought their way to a narrow victory, just as the Tigers, with the young George Ford to the fore at outside half, outlasted Sarries and relieved them of their title.

All of which left us with a final pairing of contrasting styles: Leicester's high-powered physicality, symbolised as much by the Tuilagi brothers in the backs as by the likes of Marcos Ayerza and Dan Cole up front, against the fast, more fluid rugby practised by Harlequins. The try count finished two apiece but, perhaps as most neutrals wished on the grounds that variety is the spice of life, Quins were the better side – and Robshaw, at the hub of everything, was the best of Quins, wrong-footing the heavy hitters in the Leicester defence with clever short passes at close quarters.

FACING PAGE Joe Marler, Quins' 'bristling young prop'.

BELOW Leicester's George Ford runs away from Saracens' Owen Farrell and Charlie Hodgson in the semi-final at Welford Road, which the Tigers won 24-15.

O'Shea, understandably delighted, talked afterwards of building on the foundations of his club's first title and creating something long-lasting. Everyone says something similar on these occasions – Nigel Wray, the Saracens owner, had expressed precisely the same sentiment a year previously – but with the Quins academy performing as well as any in the country, rugby could be on the verge of a 'London age'. After all, the new season will see five clubs from the capital in the top echelon, even if only one of them plays in town.

Tigers Turn Up Trumps
the 2011-12 LV= Cup

by PAUL BOLTON

'Tries from flanker Steve Mafi and wing Scott Hamilton gave Leicester the cushion they needed to withstand 15 minutes of Northampton pressure in the final quarter'

The venue may have been neutral, but the contest was as frenetic and ferocious as any of the East Midlands derbies that had preceded it. Leicester's 26-14 win over Northampton at Worcester's Sixways Stadium secured them the first major trophy of the season, but the final was marred by controversy. Northampton flanker Calum Clark was cited for breaking Leicester hooker Rob Hawkins' right elbow by hyperextending the arm. Hawkins left the field in obvious distress and missed the rest of the season, although Leicester rewarded the progress he had made before the final by awarding him a new contract.

The incident was caught by the television cameras, and Clark, who was confronted by Leicester's director of rugby Richard Cockerill at the end of the match, was later suspended. The ban ended

FACING PAGE Tongan back-row forward Steve Mafi heads for the line to score Leicester's first try against Northampton in the final at Worcester's Sixways.

RIGHT Tigers and former England prop Julian White, who retired at the end of the season and was unused from the bench on the day, lifts the LV= Cup for Leicester.

Clark's hopes of making England's summer tour to South Africa after he had broken into Stuart Lancaster's elite squad.

Hawkins' injury marred an otherwise fiercely contested affair between the old rivals, who almost slugged themselves to a standstill in their first meeting in a cup final. Tries from Tonga international flanker Steve Mafi and former All Blacks wing Scott Hamilton (the latter score a long-range interception) gave Leicester the cushion they needed to withstand 15 minutes of Saints pressure in the final quarter. Northampton spurned penalty kicks at goal, instead opting to attempt to batter Leicester into submission with a series of scrums. But Leicester turned over three of those scrums and when Northampton had a sniff of a try-scoring opportunity, Mafi got back to snaffle Scott Armstrong's pass which was intended for Paul Diggin.

'It was a fierce day, I'm sure it was a great spectacle for the neutrals to watch – if there were any in the stadium,' said Cockerill.

'As regards the trophy it's Leicester v Northampton, it's the first time we have met in a final in 130-odd years and it's one that we didn't want hanging round our necks for losing.

'Fair play to the lads, they should take the credit because they have been fantastic. We qualify for the Heineken Cup which is a bonus, we get a trophy, everyone can stop asking me whether I am under pressure for my job and we can all go home happy.'

At the start of the season the LV= Cup was low on Leicester's list of priorities, but it gained significance after they lost five of their first six Premiership matches while most of their front-line players were on World Cup duty and they failed to progress beyond the group stage of the Heineken Cup. Leicester were trounced 31-3 by the Scarlets in their opening LV= Cup match in October with a bare-bones team, but their campaign gathered momentum the following week when they were bolstered by World Cup returnees and they thrashed defending champions Gloucester 40-14 at Welford Road.

The Anglo-Welsh competition gave Leicester the chance to give first-team exposure to some of their talented youngsters, and none grasped the opportunity more firmly than George Ford, the IRB Junior Player of the Year in 2011. The precociously talented teenage fly half shone in the semi-final win at Bath and kept his place for the final even though Toby Flood was fit and available.

Having been given the chance to showcase his talent at Sixways, Ford did not disappoint, with a mature and masterful display. He created space by throwing out some clever long passes, he relieved pressure with intelligent clearance kicks and he landed important goals under pressure. Ford's 16-point haul included four penalties, the first three of which settled Leicester after

Northampton had dominated the early scrums. Leicester's scrum improved after Marcos Ayerza replaced the injured Boris Stankovich after only 11 minutes, and Mafi's try, after Ford had unleashed Geordan Murphy with another long pass, gave them the initiative. Hamilton then picked off a floated pass from Stephen Myler on his own 22 and galloped away for the deciding try. Christian Day's late effort for Saints came too late to stifle Leicester's celebrations.

'In the first half we didn't look after the ball enough, we never got to the third or fourth phase and lost it too quickly,' said Northampton director of rugby Jim Mallinder.

The Leicester team were joined on the pitch at the end by their England quartet of Tom Croft, Ben Youngs, Manu Tuilagi and Dan Cole, but it was Julian White, the veteran former England prop who retired at the end of the season, who was given the honour of lifting the trophy. 'He's been a great servant, he's a good bloke and I'm delighted he was part of this,' said Cockerill.

Bath had emerged from the group stage with the only unbeaten record and as favourites to win the competition for the first time since 1996. Their group wins included a 46-14 demolition of a depleted Northampton at the Rec, but they were punished for a sleepy performance in the semi-finals and were edged out 17-16 by an inexperienced Leicester side.

Northampton beat the Scarlets 27-12 in their semi-final at Franklin's Gardens, where forward power helped them avenge a Heineken Cup defeat by the Welsh regional side earlier in the season. England flanker

FACING PAGE Wing Scott Armstrong beats Dan Newton's covering tackle to score the Saints' second try in their 27-12 semi-final win over the Scarlets.

BELOW Newcastle's Mark Wilson takes on the Tigers in round four. Blizzard conditions greeted the Falcons, under Leicester old boy John Wells, to Welford Road, where they lost 24-13.

Tom Wood made his first appearance for Northampton in two months following his recovery from a foot injury. Wood played in the final seven days later but did not last the season.

Gloucester began their title defence with a 58-27 win over Sale at Kingsholm, where they were strengthened by the return of Scott Lawson, Alasdair Strokosch, Rory Lawson and Jim Hamilton from World Cup duty with Scotland. But the heavy defeat at Leicester mentioned above left the holders with no margin for error and six penalties from London Irish's Tom Homer sentenced them to a 23-15 defeat at the Madejski Stadium which ended their hopes of making the semi-finals.

Newcastle, who were beaten finalists in 2011, enjoyed comfortable home wins over Cardiff and Sale but were beaten at London Irish and in a blizzard at Leicester. The defeat at Welford Road marked a return to club coaching for John Wells, the former England forwards coach, who was criticised in the leaked report into England's failed World Cup campaign. Wells's first involvement with Newcastle came against a club he had captained and coached with distinction. Wells was recruited by Newcastle's locum director of rugby Gary Gold and extended his stay at Kingston Park under Gold's replacement Dean Richards.

Saracens beat Newport Gwent Dragons without kicking a ball in anger in their group match at Rodney Parade. The match was postponed because of a frozen pitch, and competition organisers awarded the tie to Saracens with a notional 20-0 scoreline after it was deemed that no suitable alternative arrangements to play the match had been put in place. The Dragons were also fined £10,000, a punishment that will be suspended until the end of the 2012-13 group stage.

Saracens were also fined, in their case £5000 but again suspended until the completion of next season's group matches, after they included the ineligible Michael Tagicakibau in their match-day squad for the group match against Worcester.

No Stopping Leinster the 2011-12 Heineken Cup

by DAVID HANDS

'The size of Leinster's victory at Twickenham – this was the biggest winning margin in a final – suggests Ulster were not at the races. Far from it: they played a full part'

The debate had begun even before Leinster claimed their third Heineken Cup in four years. Is the Irish province the best side to have played in the 17 years of European competition: better than Toulouse, who have been the perennial benchmark; better than Leicester in their pomp a decade earlier; better than Munster, whose passion plays bring so much to each passing tournament?

Context is all in such debates. Toulouse, after all, have won the cup on four occasions and appeared in two losing finals, spread over 15 seasons, making them indisputably the most successful club in tournament history. If ever there has been a team which every year under the coaching of Guy Novès is expected to challenge for the top honour, it is Toulouse.

But is the absolute best of those Toulouse sides better than the Leinstermen who have dominated Europe these last four years? The shape and balance of the squad that beat Ulster 42-14 at Twickenham on 19 May, before a record crowd of 81,744, is hard to argue against. Leinster had, moreover, reached the final by virtue of beating star-studded Clermont Auvergne in the Bordeaux semi-final, a display of character if ever there was one, even if the French side felt bereft after a

last-ditch tackle by Gordon D'Arcy jolted the ball from Wesley Fofana's grasp as the young centre was in the act of touching down for the try that would have won the match.

The size of Leinster's victory at Twickenham – this was the biggest winning margin in a final – suggests Ulster were not at the races. Far from it: they played a full part but did not offer the individual match winners with which Leinster were replete. If Sean O'Brien led the way, then Rob Kearney, later named European player of the year; Jonathan Sexton, the 2011 match winner who kicked 15 points here; and the ageless Brian O'Driscoll, who missed the pool rounds because of injury, were not far behind.

Joe Schmidt, as head coach, has added greater finesse to Leinster's play and the ruthlessness that all the great sides possess. Three Ruan Pienaar penalties and Dan Tuohy's second-half try for Ulster, reducing the margin to ten points, suggested there might be hope, but in the final quarter, Leinster scored 18 points, the last two of their five tries (another record for a final) coming when Stefan Terblanche, Ulster's full back, was in the sin-bin. Remarkably for a side blessed with such talent in the back division, four tries were scored by the forwards – O'Brien, Cian Healy, Heinke van der Merwe and Sean Cronin – and the fifth was a penalty try.

The great virtue of this Leinster team, though, is that they are not overdependent on overseas talent. Yes, they had Isa Nacewa on the wing, a World Cup winner from New Zealand in Brad Thorn at lock, Richardt Strauss from South Africa at hooker, but the heart of the side is truly Irish. This makes it all the stranger that this season's Heineken Cup did not relate more closely to form in the Six Nations Championship: Ireland produced the two Heineken Cup finalists and a quarter-finalist (Munster), yet finished in mid-table mediocrity in the championship.

Wales, winners of the Grand Slam, offered only one Heineken Cup quarter-finalist, and Cardiff Blues were blown away 34-3 in Dublin – by Leinster. New-look England, recovering from a disastrous World Cup campaign, under new management and green as grass, came second in the Six Nations on the back of one of the worst European campaigns by their clubs, in which only Saracens reached the last eight and found that home advantage mattered little when faced with the all-round excellence of Clermont Auvergne.

ABOVE Wesley Fofana gets the ball over the try line for Clermont Auvergne late in the semi-final against Leinster but loses control of it in the tackle. No try!

FACING PAGE Leinster celebrate Sean O'Brien's try after 12 minutes of the final against Ulster at Twickenham.

The English and French clubs also provided a rumble of thunder during the second half of the season. Not for the first time, they sought change to the tournament structure to provide that perceived sporting essential – a level playing field. Their complaints created a disconcerting backdrop, but nothing should detract from Leinster's achievement in going through Europe unbeaten and becoming only the second side (after Leicester in 2001 and 2002) to secure back-to-back titles. The only hiccough came in round one when a penalty from the touch line by Sexton with the last kick of the game was needed to secure a 16-16 draw in Montpellier. In 2012-13 Leinster will have the opportunity to extend that unbeaten run beyond 15 games.

If the initial joust provided a few upsets, it was hardly surprising. The tournament opened a month later than usual, in mid-November, to allow the echoes of the 2011 World Cup in New Zealand to die away. Scotland had failed to reach the last eight in the global tournament, but Edinburgh, who went on to reach the semi-finals for the first time, and Glasgow Warriors disposed of well-regarded opponents from England, London Irish (in Reading) and Bath respectively.

But the club that suffered most, perhaps, was Northampton, the beaten 2011 finalists. They felt they had done enough to claim a notable victory over Munster at Thomond Park when they led 21-20 with the clock ticking deep into time added on; but, as he has done so often before, Ronan O'Gara had the last word. The fly half watched his colleagues sustain play through 41 phases before the position was achieved from which he dropped a winning goal with the last kick of the match.

Just to prove it was no fluke, O'Gara did it again the following weekend to give Munster their 27-24 win at Castres. But this was not to be another of Munster's captivating trawls through Europe. They did top Pool One, but their dreams died in a quarter-final in their own backyard when Ulster showed how much they had learned from scrapping with Leicester and Clermont Auvergne in Pool Four, and from the strong South African presence in their midst.

Arguably the defining pool game was Ulster's 41-7 win over Leicester at Ravenhill on the penultimate weekend of qualifying. Leicester had suffered something similar in 2004, losing 33-0 in

Belfast, but this defeat ensured they would fail to reach the last eight. Pienaar, the Springbok scrum half, punished their every indiscretion to register 21 points and Andrew Trimble scored two of their four tries. Ulster could not oust Clermont Auvergne from top spot, but a losing bonus point from a 19-15 defeat at the Stade Marcel Michelin confirmed them as serious contenders.

More serious, as it happened, than Toulouse. If one result confirmed the inconsistencies of England's clubs, it was Gloucester's 34-24 win over Toulouse at Kingsholm in Pool Six, which gave Harlequins the chance to progress if they could beat Connacht in Galway, but, in mud and rain, the club that were to become English champions could not. Gloucester played outstanding rugby, their young backs ripping Toulouse to shreds to score four tries; no one could have foreseen that, thereafter, their domestic season would collapse in a heap.

It left Saracens, whose ambitious plan to play a Heineken Cup pool game with Biarritz in Cape Town fell foul of local politics in the Cape, as England's only quarter-finalists. Once they had lost 22-3 to Clermont, though, there was no English representative in either European competition at the semi-final stage – the first time this had happened. Nor could Toulouse join Clermont in the last four, losing 19-14 at Murrayfield, where a record crowd of 37,881 for a European tie in Scotland urged on an Edinburgh side inspired from fly half by Greig Laidlaw.

Hard though they tried, Edinburgh could not take the final step. Their hands let them down in Dublin against Ulster, Pienaar added 17 points to his European swag and the Irish province's 22-19 win carried them to their first final for 13 years. Leinster, however, made sure that, in the fifth final involving teams from the same country, there could be only one winner.

ABOVE Gloucester full back Jonny May sprints away to score one of his two tries in the Cherry and Whites' 34-24 round six home win over Toulouse.

FACING PAGE The cruellest blow. Ronan O'Gara sinks Northampton with a dropped goal from the final play after an extraordinary feat of ball retention by Munster.

PAGES 104-105 A third Heineken Cup title in four years for Leinster.

Biarritz Grab Chance
the 2011-12 Amlin Challenge Cup by HUGH GODWIN

'Yachvili dropped to his knees, pointing the index finger of each hand to the heavens. Wilkinson, typically, pulled the merest of grimaces and offered a congratulatory hand'

ABOVE Full-time at the Stoop, and Biarritz have won the 2011-12 Amlin Challenge Cup.

The sometimes lukewarm attitude demonstrated by French clubs towards the second-tier European Challenge Cup turned red hot when the Top 14 supplied all four semi-finalists, and ultimately a drumskin-tight 21-18 victory for Biarritz Olympique over Toulon in the final played, inconveniently in an obvious respect, at Harlequins' Twickenham Stoop. The easiest correlation to infer is between the high wages and great strength in depth of the playing squads in France and their domination of the Amlin-sponsored competition that comprises, each year, the also-rans from the previous season's club championships around the continent. Unless, perhaps, they just got collectively lucky?

Either way, this was also the third year of the twist in the Amlin tale of admitting the third-, fourth- and fifth-best-performing pool runners-up from the concurrent Heineken Cup into the quarter-finals of the Challenge Cup. As a result, Harlequins, who had slipped up against Connacht in the major event, were offered a roundabout route to defending the Amlin title they had won in

Cardiff in 2011. But neither Quins nor the Scarlets, who also arrived from the Heineken, went any further, losing away ties in the last eight to Toulon (37-8) and Brive (15-11) respectively.

The third wild-card entry belonged to Biarritz, and theirs was a different story. Finishing the French league season only ninth, the perennial Heineken Cup participants from the sublime surfing town on the sunny Atlantic seaboard strove hard to reach the Challenge Cup final, knowing they needed to win it if they were to qualify for the premier competition for a thirteenth consecutive season. Odd that the greatest prize in a tournament is to avoid it next time around, but such is the set-up in Europe.

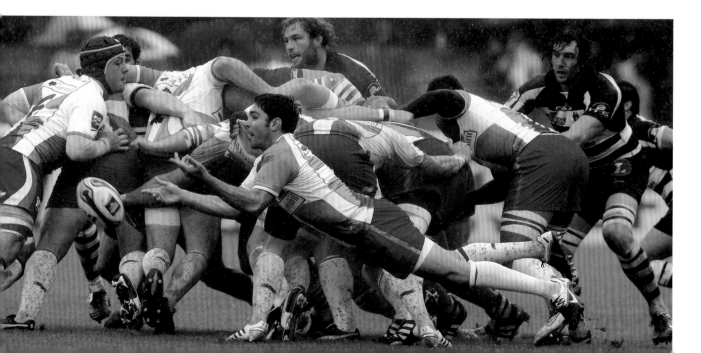

The sponsors' statistical analysis pointed to Biarritz enjoying an advantage over Toulon in defence, kicking and line out. There was enduring quality in the Basque club's personnel, from the USA flyer 'Zee' Ngwenya on the wing and still-effervescent former England full back Iain Balshaw to the redoubtable scrum half Dimitri Yachvili and No. 8 Imanol Harinordoquy.

These luminaries were nevertheless viewed as travelling to London in the shade of Toulon's cosmopolitans, who had eliminated Jonny Wilkinson's old club Newcastle, along with Lyon and Petrarca, in Pool Two. Wilkinson, who had retired from Test rugby in mid-season, was chasing both his and the club's first European title (he had gone off injured during Toulon's losing Challenge Cup final against Cardiff Blues in 2010). Matt Giteau, the gifted Wallaby midfield back, made his European club debut when Toulon inflicted a Friday-night demolition on Harlequins, who had won an important Premiership match against Saracens at Wembley the previous Saturday and were missing their England captain Chris Robshaw and All Black fly half Nick Evans.

Five penalties by Wilkinson and a conversion of France centre Mathieu Bastareaud's try had Toulon 22-3 ahead of Quins at half-time. Giteau then kicked five points and Benjamin Lapeyre and Steffon Armitage, the 26-year-old England flanker who had joined Toulon the previous summer from London Irish, scored tries. Indeed, Armitage scored another try early in the home semi-final win over Stade Français, but this was a shoddy shoot-themselves-in-the-foot effort by the multi-millionaires, belying the big-time experience of Carl Hayman, Joe van Niekerk and the like. While the injury-hit Stade fielded the great Australian flanker George Smith at centre, having knocked out first-time participants Exeter Chiefs in a desperately tight quarter-final in Paris, it required a Wilkinson dropped goal following on from three missed kicks to take Toulon to the final, 32-29.

The former France coach Bernard Laporte had been tasked by moneybags owner Mourad Boudjellal with piecing together the expensive Toulon jigsaw. 'Bernard has brought his own distinctive game plan with him,' said Armitage, who grew up in the south of France and played with his brothers in Nice. 'Although Toulon are regarded as big spenders, he also makes sure that everyone keeps their feet on the ground and everyone is equal.'

A latter-day Orwell may have observed that while all the Toulonnais were equal, Wilkinson was more equal than others, but Biarritz had no inferiority complex when it came to kicking. Their own sharpshooter, Yachvili, accumulated 30 points across the 26-23 quarter-final win away to Wasps and 19-0 defeat of Brive in the last four at home at the Parc des Sports Aguiléra. In the latter match the only try was scored by the long-serving centre Damien Traille.

So with the pool stages out of the way (273,167 spectators overall watched the group matches, a 17 per cent increase on the 2010-11 figure of 233,598) and the last eight reduced to two, the final was played on the eve of the Heineken Cup showdown at nearby Twickenham. Biarritz president and über-luminary Serge Blanco wished for a better result than the Heineken final defeats of 2006 and 2010; and indeed the conclusion to his own brilliant playing career, a defeat by Toulon in the 1992 French Championship final. 'As far as our Top 14 position is concerned sometimes we have a big headache and the following week everything is better,' Blanco said of his frustratingly inconsistent side. '[But] our team is better now than it was two months ago. It is the proof that without the World Cup and then with a complete squad the season would have been different.' A dedicated Facebook page and '#AmlinCCFinal' Twitter tag reflected new means of publicity, but the match was old-fashioned red-raw rugby from the off.

To a backdrop of brass-band boisterousness from the 'BO' supporters, the stick-legged Yachvili kicked the Basques 3-0 ahead after four minutes; Wilkinson's left boot levelled after 11. And tit for tat they went, with runs by Ngwenya and Giteau among the passages of play generally halted by a fierce contest for the ball on the floor and blasts of English referee Wayne Barnes's whistle: 6-3 to Biarritz, 6-6, 9-6, 9-9, 12-9 at half-time. Hoary promises not to allow the expert kickers sight of the posts died, as they often do, when the trophy came in sight.

Van Niekerk was tipped over leaping for a line out thrown by Sébastien Bruno to allow Wilkinson to square the scores a fourth time in the 44th minute. Soon afterwards came a moment of violent

ABOVE The final at the Stoop. Jonny Wilkinson of Toulon stands by to tackle Biarritz prop Eugene van Staden.

FACING PAGE Winning skipper Imanol Harinordoquy celebrates with the Biarritz faithful.

contention. The sidestepping Ngwenya ran into the bulky Hayman who flipped the Zimbabwean-American over without quite driving him into the ground: a half-tip tackle, it might be concluded by viewing the TV replays, though Barnes of course had only one look and showed the New Zealander only a yellow card. Yachvili, 30 metres or so from the posts, kicked for 15-12. A sorry few minutes for Toulon continued with Armitage sent to join Hayman in the sin-bin for entering the side of a ruck under the posts, and with Yachvili's sixth penalty it was 18-12 to Biarritz after 53 minutes.

Hayman harrumphed back into action, with English lock Dean Schofield heaving behind him, to pulverise Biarritz at a scrum – and Wilkinson halved the deficit. On 65 minutes, it was 18-18, with Wilkinson corkscrewing a lofty drop at goal to its target. The next chance was yielded by a struggling Biarritz scrum, but Wilkinson was short from just inside his own half. And there would have been a much better one, closer in, if the officials had not missed a sly ankle tap from a heinously offside, prone Yachvili on his opposite number, Sébastien Tillous-Borde, that put the Toulon No. 9 off his pass – a penalty and probably a yellow card luckily avoided by the Biarritz linchpin.

With eight minutes to play, Alexis Palisson fielded a high kick, and Traille's crunching tackle forced a penalty by isolating the Toulon right wing as he went to ground. Yachvili goaled for 21-18, leaving Toulon on the brink. The clock showed 79½ minutes as they were awarded a penalty, and Wilkinson hurried forward to find touch 30-odd metres from the goal line. The line out was won, but in the ninth phase of possession Toulon were done for by a blundering obstruction as flankers Pierrick Gunther and Armitage attempted to drive into the Biarritz 22 and set up a penalty or a drop. Traille's squeals of delight came over loud and clear through Barnes's ref-mic; Yachvili dropped to his knees, pointing the index finger of each hand to the heavens. Wilkinson, typically, pulled the merest of grimaces and offered a congratulatory hand.

Harinordoquy said: 'Jonny Wilkinson has given a hard time to me in the past and he has done it to Dimitri as well – but tonight it was Dimitri who gave Toulon a difficult time.' And in chaotic but rather heartwarming scenes as ecstatic Basques surrounded him on the pitch, the Biarritz captain lifted the 2012 Amlin Challenge Cup.

EVANS
property group

**The Evans Property Group
is pleased to support the
splendid work done by
Wooden Spoon**

REVIEW OF THE
SEASON 2011-12

Wales's Three in Eight
the 2012 Six Nations Championship
by CHRIS JONES

'Wales led 10-3 at the break thanks to winger Alex Cuthbert's superb individual try, but France remained firmly in the game, with two Welsh penalties hitting the woodwork'

There is always an air of uncertainty leading into the RBS 6 Nations Championship following a Rugby World Cup, and that only added to the excitement of a tournament that ended with Wales surviving a ferocious onslaught from France in Cardiff to allow captain Sam Warburton to raise the trophy and signal a third Grand Slam in just eight years. It went some way to easing the hurt felt by the Welsh players and the entire nation after their semi-final loss in the World Cup to France, who then just failed to stop the All Blacks becoming world champions. That match signalled the end of Marc Lièvremont's reign as French coach and the baton was handed over to Philippe Saint-André, who introduced some new talent into a side that was still capable of underachieving.

Wales benefited greatly from the excellence of their coaching group headed by Warren Gatland, and they all played key roles in a campaign that saw England and Italy feature new head coaches with very different results. For England, Stuart Lancaster was appointed as interim head coach following the World Cup debacle that cost Martin Johnson his job. Only Graham Rowntree retained his role with the forwards, with Andy Farrell being loaned to England by Saracens to take charge of the backs – a full-time job he would initially turn down before changing his mind and becoming part of the set-up again.

The Six Nations would become one long job interview for Lancaster and he handled himself and the playing squad so well the Rugby Football Union gave him the role full-time. Italy waved goodbye to Nick Mallett, who was the only other candidate shortlisted for the England job, and asked Frenchman Jacques Brunel to take over. While he avoided the Wooden Spoon, it was another season of toil for the Azzurri.

Bottom spot was reserved for the infuriatingly inconsistent Scots, who gave head coach Andy

RIGHT It's Grand Slam Wales again after winning the rematch of the RWC 2011 semi-final against France 16-9 in Cardiff.

Robinson another championship in which he was seen banging various inanimate objects in the coach's box as try-scoring chances were thrown away – most notably in the opening game against England, when two-on-ones weren't even good enough to allow the Scots to reach the line.

The championship would also finish on a sad note with a minute's silence being observed to mark the death of Lions and Wales legend Mervyn Davies, who led his country to Slam glory in 1976. It was fitting that the Welsh players honoured the great man by clinching the Slam again.

On the opening day, Saint-André's reign with France got off to a winning start with a 30-12 win over Italy at the Stade de France. The Clermont trio of Aurélien Rougerie, Julien Malzieu and Wesley Fofana, the last-mentioned on debut, all scored tries, while Toulouse flyer Vincent Clerc also touched down. Kris Burton added nine points for Italy, with replacement Tobias Botes kicking a further penalty, but in the end the French had been too strong in attack and defence.

Charlie Hodgson's charge-down try and eight points from Owen Farrell were enough to allow Lancaster to enjoy an opening 13-6 win at Murrayfield. Harlequins' Chris Robshaw became captain with Tom Wood injured and out of contention. It was a new-look England team and they played with a passion and commitment that impressed everyone, and showed that Lancaster had erased many of the problems created during the World Cup.

Robinson knew the pressure would be on his experienced side and it showed as they were unable to score a try despite enjoying possession and territorial advantage. One of the few high points was the arrival on the Test scene of David Denton, who would become one of the form back-row players of the Six Nations.

Over in Dublin, a fingernail-biting match ended with Leigh Halfpenny kicking a last-minute penalty to earn Wales a 23-21 victory over Ireland at the Aviva Stadium. Gatland's side had twice led through a Jonathan Davies try in each half, but Ireland hit back on both occasions – first through Rory Best's try and then a Tommy Bowe score with 13 minutes left on the clock.

There was a further twist in the rematch of the World Cup quarter-final when the outstanding George North went over in the corner, but Halfpenny missed a kick to edge Wales back in front. However, the full back made no mistake when flanker Stephen Ferris was sin-binned for a tip tackle with just seconds remaining. Ferris' yellow card was not the only talking point, with Bradley Davies being binned rather than shown the red card for what looked a far worse offence with 15 minutes left. Captain Warburton suffered a leg injury and didn't take part in the second half, and injury would blight his championship, including the final game with France. Justin Tipuric made his Six Nations debut as replacement in Dublin and would prove to be a more than able deputy.

BELOW Without Leigh Halfpenny's last-minute penalty, Wales's Grand Slam dream would have died on the first weekend in Dublin.

FACING PAGE England give chase in vain as Tommaso Benvenuti runs away to score Italy's second try in Rome.

England made it two wins from two in snow-hit Rome. Once the Stadio Olimpico pitch had been cleared, they battled past Italy 19-15 to continue their perfect start. Hodgson's second charge-down try in two games plus Farrell's kicking was enough for another narrow success in a match that Italy knew they could and should have won. However, like the Scots, the Azzurri could not put England away, and this dogged determination was to serve England well throughout the campaign.

Two first-half penalties from Farrell gave England a 6-0 lead, but tries from Giovanbattista Venditti and Tommaso Benvenuti before the break brought the Italians back into it, and they led 12-6 at half-time. Hodgson's try at the start of the second half got England going again, and two more penalties from Farrell were enough as they held on for the win.

Leigh Halfpenny was again the star of the show as Wales turned on the second-half power to beat Scotland 27-13 at the Millennium Stadium. Halfpenny, who continued to prove that size isn't everything in modern rugby, finished with two tries for an individual haul of 22 points. Centre Nick De Luca and full back Rory Lamont of Scotland both collected yellow cards after the break and Wales took full advantage with an Alex Cuthbert try. Robinson's men did end their international try-scoring drought late on as Greig Laidlaw dived over, but the damage was done. Warburton pulled out of the match, which gave Aaron Shingler his first cap.

Jonathan Sexton, still trying to convince doubters he is Ireland's future at No. 10, was impressive in his country's 42-10 win over Italy. The Leinster fly half kicked 17 points at the Aviva Stadium as two scores from Tommy Bowe, a Keith Earls try and late efforts from Tom Court and Andrew Trimble halted a run of three consecutive home defeats. Italy had skipper Sergio Parisse to thank for their try, but scrum half Tobias Botes, making his first international start not at No. 9 but in the No. 10 jersey, was able to convert just two of five shots at goal. With Ireland clear, Ronan O'Gara replaced Gordon D'Arcy to win a record 118th cap.

Scott Williams, putting together a run of form that suggests he could be a Lions Test certainty next year, came up with the late try that sealed a 19-12 Wales win against England at Twickenham. The Scarlets centre replaced the injured Jamie Roberts at half-time and won the game when he stole the ball from Courtney Lawes in midfield before kicking and chasing to cross for the decisive score. England had hoped 12 points from the boot of Farrell would be good enough for a win, but that try and 14 points from Leigh Halfpenny ultimately saw Wales lift the Triple Crown on English soil for the first time.

France, having had their match with Ireland postponed because of a frozen pitch, continued their successful start, but were given a real scare by Scotland at Murrayfield before running out 23-17 winners. Stuart Hogg scored early on his home debut as the Scots led 10-0 after 25 minutes, but France worked their way back into it thanks to a second try in as many Tests from Wesley Fofana

*Fig. 1: Typical Six Nations P*ROFITS *(hoping for some tries)*

Discipline, intense concentration and effort – sound familiar? All these elements are just as important on the Profit hunting ground as they are on the rugby pitch.

If you'd like to find out more about Hunting Profits please contact your financial adviser, call 0800 092 2051 or visit artemis.co.uk.

ARTEMIS
The PROFIT Hunter

The value of an investment, and any income from it, can fall as well as rise as a result of market and currency fluctuations and you may not get back the amount originally invested. Please remember that past performance is not a guide to the future.

Issued by Artemis Fund Managers Ltd which is authorised and regulated by the Financial Services Authority (www.fsa.gov.uk), 25 The North Colonnade, Canary Wharf, London E14 5HS.

and the boot of Morgan Parra. Lee Jones's first try in Scottish colours had put the home side back in front 15-13 after 55 minutes, but Maxime Médard hit back and Lionel Beauxis added a dropped goal.

When the postponed fixture against Ireland took place, it turned out that wing Tommy Bowe's first-half double was in vain as France denied the visitors a first win in Paris for 12 years, coming back to draw 17-17 at the Stade de France. The original match had been called off ludicrously late, with the players already out and the band ready to play the anthems. It was a dreadful scenario, which damaged the credibility of the tournament and left Irish fans fuming, having paid a lot of money to make it to Paris.

Going into the interval 17-6 ahead, thanks to the two Bowe tries and goals from Jonathan Sexton, Ireland hoped to secure a first victory in the French capital since 2000, but after Morgan Parra had kept France in it, the impressive Wesley Fofana crossed after the break to cap a fine revival from the home side. Nevertheless, their dreams of an RBS 6 Nations Grand Slam vanished as they failed to find the winning score in the dying minutes.

Wales made the most of France's inability to keep winning, second-half tries from Jamie Roberts and Alex Cuthbert seeing off Italy 24-3 to keep their own Grand Slam hopes alive. Needless to say, there were another 11 points from the boot of Leigh Halfpenny. Meanwhile, in Dublin, stand-in skipper Rory Best celebrated his temporary appointment in perfect style by crossing for one of Ireland's four scores in a 32-14 win that condemned Scotland to a fourth consecutive defeat. Hooker Best took charge in the absence of Paul O'Connell, injured, and with regular Ireland skipper Brian O'Driscoll taking no part in the 2012 championship. Ireland's other tries came from Eoin Reddan, Andrew Trimble and Fergus McFadden, while Jonathan Sexton kicked 12 points. Scotland more than held their own in the first half, with a try from Richie Gray and three Greig Laidlaw penalties. However, they didn't score again after the interval.

BELOW Making his home Test debut, full back Stuart Hogg flies in for Scotland after seven minutes of the match against France at Murrayfield.

In Paris, Lancaster put down a sizeable marker as his young side upset an experienced French team 24-22. First-half tries from Manu Tuilagi and Ben Foden set the tone for a memorable England showing, while flanker Tom Croft added a score after the turnaround as Lancaster's men recovered from their Twickenham defeat to Wales to keep hold of their slim title hopes. With more than three times as many caps to their names as England, France were expected to repeat their recent winning performance at the World Cup and overturn the visitors. However, Tuilagi produced a moment of magic out of nothing for a solo score and then Ben Morgan fed Foden on the French 22, and the Northampton full back forced his way over the French try line.

England then gave away silly penalties and were on the ropes when Leicester flanker Croft produced a rabbit out of the hat with ten minutes remaining, breaking the French line to score in the corner after rounding last man Clément Poitrenaud with a sidestep. With less than ten minutes left, replacement Phil Dowson demonstrated immense bravery on the line to hold the opposition up, but from the resulting scrum Fofana went over. In the end England survived – just.

In Cardiff on the final weekend, Wales were made to sweat all the way for their 16-9 victory by a determined France side. Wales led 10-3 at the break thanks to winger Alex Cuthbert's superb individual try, but France remained firmly in the game, with two Welsh penalties hitting the woodwork. A further penalty from Dimitri Yachvili plus one from Lionel Beauxis meant Wales once again needed Halfpenny's boot to help win their third Grand Slam in eight years. England secured second place thanks to a dominant performance from their scrum, which laid the platform for a 30-9 victory over Ireland. England dismantled the Ireland front row, resulting in a second-half penalty try, while Farrell contributed 20 points. Replacement scrum half Ben Youngs scored a 74th-minute try from a quickly taken tap penalty – and Lancaster finished with four wins.

Giovanbattista Venditti's try just after half-time gave Italy their maiden win under coach Brunel and condemned Scotland to a 13-6 defeat and a first Wooden Spoon since 2007. Despite being on the back foot for nearly the whole of the first half, Scotland managed to get into half-time at 3-3, with Greig Laidlaw's penalty cancelling out the effort of Mirco Bergamasco, who missed with two other kicks. But Venditti's try while centre Nick De Luca was in the sin-bin gave Italy an advantage they would not relinquish at a sold-out Stadio Olimpico. It concluded a fascinating Six Nations – but don't we say that every year!

> **BELOW** Having destroyed the Ireland scrummage, the England forwards, led by the front row, celebrate a second-half penalty try at Twickenham.

The Club Scene
England: The Welsh Arrive
by ALASTAIR EYKYN

'The annual Army v Navy match was played in front of a record crowd of 65,302, who braved the rain to witness the Army lift the prestigious Babcock Trophy'

Whilst a combination of stubborn resilience and bloody-mindedness saw London Welsh into the Premiership after the mother of all political and legal scraps, there were other Championship clubs rather less pleased with the season's outcome. For a long time, Bristol looked the likely contenders to return to the top flight. Liam Middleton's men were the regular season winners, finishing a healthy seven points clear at the top of the table. For all their consistency, though, the elaborate Championship play-off system, and the Cornish Pirates, did for them. In the semi-finals, Bristol came unstuck against the Cornishmen by an aggregate score of 63-53, largely as a result of a big 45-24 Pirates win at the Mennaye Field in the opening leg. Once again, Bedford Blues had an impressive campaign, but they too were undone at the semi-final stage. Despite winning the second leg 24-17 at Old Deer Park, the Blues were edged out by London Welsh by an aggregate of 30 points to 27.

BELOW All smiles for London Welsh as they win the 2012 Championship play-offs. Skipper Jon Mills holds the trophy and is flanked to his right by club chairman Bleddyn Phillips.

At the bottom of the Championship, Esher and London Scottish became involved in a relegation shoot-out. Esher won a paltry four league games in the regular season, and just two in their relegation pool matches. In their final match away to Scottish, they scored five tries in a 31-26 win in front of a crowd of 2000 supporters, but they were powerless to alter their fate. Mike Schmid's team were sent back down to National League One where they triumphed two years ago. Esher chairman of rugby John Inverdale was quick to accept the situation. 'We were bottom of the league,' he said, 'and we were a club who have campaigned for the bottom side to go down without play-offs, so we have no argument.'

So whilst Esher prepared for a reduction in funding, and life in National One, a very different club moved in the opposite direction. In fact, Jersey RFC have been moving upwards at a rate of knots for several years now, and their tale of success is one to gladden the heart of every rugby supporter. For the fourth time in five seasons, the islanders won promotion, finishing seven points clear of Ealing Trailfinders and beating Coventry 37-13 away in the penultimate game of the season to secure their Championship future. Only seven years ago, Jersey were playing in London SW Division Three. Now they are numbered amongst England's 24 finest clubs.

After so nearly winning promotion to the Championship last season, Barking found life rather different this time around. A year ago, they were just minutes away from a place in club rugby's second tier, before London Scottish killed off their chances. This season they were relegated to National Two South after winning just seven of their 30 league matches. Promoted into National One are Loughborough Students (winners of National Two North) and Old Albanians (National Two South) – who narrowly squeezed past Richmond. Richmond eventually went up as well after a play-off win against Caldy.

Arguably the most disappointing story of the 2011-12 season was the financial collapse of Rugby Lions. As the main club in the town where rugby union was born, they have a rich history dating back 139 years. On the pitch they were irresistible. They were unbeaten for the entirety

of the season, winning promotion from National League Three Midlands. Off the pitch, though, the decline was dramatic. It culminated in the departure of their high-profile head coach Neil Back to join Edinburgh Rugby as assistant forwards coach and in the exodus of a number of senior players. The director of Rugby Lions' parent company, Michael Aland, had set his sights on achieving Premiership status within five years and the ambitious provision of a 30,000-seater stadium. However, in July 2012, the Insolvency Service confirmed the club's liquidation. The RFU 'asked the club to meet the obligations to rugby creditors of The Rugby Football Club (2011) Ltd by 5pm' on 17 August. When they were unable to do so, the RFU announced that Rugby Lions would 'play no part in the leagues in this coming season. National League Two South [to which Rugby Lions had been promoted] will continue with 15 clubs.'

Elsewhere on the English rugby scene, the annual Army v Navy match was played at Twickenham in late April in front of a record crowd of 65,302 committed supporters, who braved the rain to witness the Army lift the prestigious Babcock Trophy. The pre-match entertainment featured 100 members of the Military Wives Choir, who treated the crowd to two songs from their number one album. There followed a rousing rendition of the national anthem as the choir teamed up with the Band of the Coldstream Guards. The fallen were honoured with an emotional minute's applause, which also recognised the absentees currently serving in Afghanistan. The majority of the Army team have seen active service there.

The Army were the favourites to retain their title, but it was the Navy who struck the first blow, with an early penalty from their skipper Dave Pascoe. It was the only time they were in front. The red shirts of the Army swarmed forward, intent on bullying the opposition pack. With captain Darrell Ball dominating the line out, and the loose forwards providing the necessary fluidity, the Army squeezed the Navy. Open-side flanker Mark Lee excelled in his final game for the Army.

Despite the filthy conditions, the Army's ambition was to play an expansive style of rugby. Their back division was brilliantly marshalled by half backs Tom Chennell and Jack Prasad, the latter a Fijian international. Provided with a conveyor belt of quality possession, they launched their balanced runners out wide. Tank driver Semesa Rokoduguni lived up to his billing with a fabulous hat-trick, adding to the four tries he had scored against the RAF. His fellow wing Sam Speight also touched down, as did Darrell Ball (recently returned from Afghanistan) and David Duffus. Ceri Cummings kicked 18 points.

The Navy were comprehensively outplayed, with Pascoe's kicking providing their only points in a 48-9 defeat. Marsh Cormack battled hard at lock, but the Blues dropped off tackles and failed to secure the possession they needed. Their influential Worcester wing Josh Drauniniu cut an isolated figure. It was a high-quality display from a high-quality Army outfit.

Five months earlier, also at HQ, Oxford University had proved the stronger in a feisty 130th Varsity Match. For the first time since 2002, the Dark Blues registered consecutive victories over their Cambridge rivals, with a comfortable 28-10 win. A penalty from the tidy Cambridge fly half Steve Townend opened the scoring, before Oxford prop Will Kane rumbled over for the first try of the afternoon, converted by Cassian Bramham-Law. Then midway through the first half, the match burst into life – and controversy.

Oxford's John Hudson flung himself at full length and at high speed onto a loose ball which had crossed the try line, to deny Cambridge a score. However, a penalty try was awarded from the resulting five-metre scrum, when the Dark Blue forwards were adjudged by referee Dave Pearson to have dragged the set-piece down. Shortly beforehand, Oxford captain John Carter had been held down off the ball by his opposite number Dave Allen and punched squarely in the eye. For the first time since 1997, former university captains were serving as assistant referees, with Joe Roff (Oxford 2007) and Ross Blake (Cambridge 2007) running the lines. Neither they nor referee Pearson saw the incident, which left Carter nursing a swollen black eye.

Oxford led just 13-10 at the break but made certain of the result after half-time, scoring 15 unanswered points. The excellent lock forward Karl Outen was awarded the Alastair Hignell medal as man of the match, and his try from a catch-and-drive at the line out was the first of the second period. It was followed by a lovely score from the England Sevens star Tom Mitchell, who touched down with nine minutes remaining to complete the win. It was Oxford's biggest victory in the fixture since 1988.

Wooden Spoon
The children's charity of rugby

BEHIND SCOTTISH RUGBY.

THE FAMOUS GROUSE
SCOTLAND'S FAVOURITE WHISKY

Enjoy responsibly.
www.thefamousgrouse.com

for the facts **drinkaware.co.uk**

Scotland: A Knockout Season

by ALAN LORIMER

'Edinburgh may have been the big story, but there was, too, a buzz in the west of the country after Glasgow Warriors finished fourth in the RaboDirect PRO12'

If Scottish fans had been lukewarm in their support for professional rugby north of the border, then an event at Murrayfield in April 2012 was to signal a massive change in attitude towards the moneyed side of the game. A crowd of 38,000 got behind their club for a quarter-final of the Heineken European Cup. A new era for Edinburgh rugby had begun.

There was a sense of excitement about Edinburgh's prospects, a sense that the capital side could carry into the knockout stages the confidence that had taken the club through the pool matches, and a feeling that Edinburgh could derail the progress-by-right of Toulouse, a club operating on four times the budget of the Scottish outfit.

Edinburgh, under new coach Michael Bradley, were the underdogs for this match and, as always for a Scottish team, it suited them. But

> *BELOW* A new cap for Scotland in the 2012 Six Nations, wing Lee Jones seeks a way past Thierry Dusautoir and Lionel Beauxis as Edinburgh see off Toulouse 19-14 in the Heineken Cup quarter-finals.

from the moment Greig Laidlaw hoisted the ball deep into the Toulouse 22-metre area to create mayhem in the visitors' defence and with it the first try, Edinburgh looked winners, despite being down to 13 men at one stage with two players in the bin.

Laidlaw's accurate kicking, which included a timely dropped goal, and his commanding performance at stand-off helped Edinburgh to a sensational 19-14 win, a result that was both assisted and enjoyed by a record-breaking crowd at the international stadium.

Edinburgh then faced Ulster three weeks later in the semi-final at the Aviva Stadium in Dublin. Hopes were high among Scottish fans that Edinburgh would produce another big performance, but in the event their weakness in the front row, a mirror of Scotland's woes, cost them dearly as Ulster's powerful pack and the individual skills of Ruan Pienaar gave the province a 22-19 win.

Still, Edinburgh's run in the Heineken Cup had created a froth of excitement, whipped up by a 20-19 away win over London Irish in the first round and then a week later a sensational 48-47 victory against Racing Métro 92 at Murrayfield. A defeat to and then a win over Cardiff kept Edinburgh on track, before second-leg victories over Racing Métro 92 and Irish ensured a table-topping quarter-final qualification.

Edinburgh's Heineken Cup successes were in sharp contrast to the club's dismal second-bottom finishing place in the RaboDirect PRO12 league. But much of this sorry story can be explained by the lack of depth in the cash-strapped Edinburgh club during the World Cup and the Six Nations. The flip side of the coin, however, was that the absence of so many Scotland squad players on international duty allowed a number of talented newcomers to emerge.

Not least of these was David Denton, who wasted little time in showing Andy Robinson why he should have been in Scotland's World Cup squad. Denton, along with Laidlaw, headed a group of new stars that included young lock Grant Gilchrist, inside centre Matt Scott, winger Lee Jones, stand-offs Harry Leonard and Gregor Hunter, and full back Tom Brown.

Edinburgh may have been the big story in Scottish professional rugby, but there was, too, a buzz in the west of the country after Glasgow Warriors finished fourth in the RaboDirect PRO12 league to

earn qualification for the play-offs and with it a semi-final against Leinster in Dublin. The 19-15 win for European champions Leinster ended Glasgow's hopes of glory, but importantly the Warriors had demonstrated to the swelling number of supporters that success was within reach.

Glasgow's encouraging season was down to the emergence of a number of young players, the most prominent of which was 19-year-old Stuart Hogg, arguably the most exciting young player in Scottish rugby. As was the case at Edinburgh, it was the absence of Scotland World Cup players that opened doors for hitherto second strings to grab their chances. And they did. Duncan Weir settled in at stand-off and overtook Ruaridh Jackson; Alex Dunbar became a player to watch at centre; Chris Fusaro excited as a ball-winning open-side; Murray McConnell and Henry Pyrgos competed for the scrum-half jersey; Rob Harley consolidated his position in the back row; Tom Ryder impressed at lock; and in the front row this was the season in which Ryan Grant, Jon Welsh and Pat MacArthur emerged as international contenders.

For the 2012-13 season it's all change at Warriors, with Gregor Townsend now at the helm in place of the long-serving Sean Lineen and the Glasgow club having moved from Firhill to Scotstoun Stadium, the venue for the 2014 Commonwealth Games track-and-field programme.

Professional club rugby in Scotland could be entering a new era as the result of changes to the top echelons of the Scottish Rugby Union that have resulted in a shift away from a bean-counting approach to a more entrepreneurial culture. Previously Edinburgh and Glasgow were seen purely as the vehicles for developing Scottish talent, even if that meant the two clubs were unable to compete seriously against sides stacked with talented overseas players.

The new philosophy driven by Scottish Rugby Union CEO Mark Dodson and chairman Sir Moir Lockhead is the straightforward credo that commercial success is brought about by success on the field – which explains the investment in a number of high-profile southern hemisphere players to ensure that never again will a lack of success be blamed on a lack of depth.

Inevitably there are worries that the arrival of experienced professionals at both Edinburgh and Glasgow will limit opportunities for the next generation of young Scottish talent. That is a genuine concern and one that could be solved by the revival of a third professional team. In the meantime, the hope is that the top end of the amateur game, which for the 2012-13 season has become a more elite ten-team league, might be the path for many aspirants.

Certainly the standard of the amateur game at the top level is reassuringly high, confirmed by the ability of Scottish clubs to compete in the British & Irish Cup against professional opponents. Further proof is the ease with which certain players can step up from amateur rugby to the professional game when the situation demands. A case in point was the Currie centre Doug Fife, who made four appearances for Edinburgh and in one of them collected the man-of-the-match award.

His club were expected to challenge hard for the Premiership title, but ultimately Currie were overtaken by ambitious

LEFT 'Arguably the most exciting young player in Scottish rugby', Stuart Hogg sails over Andrew Conway to score for Glasgow Warriors against Leinster in the RaboDirect PRO12 play-off. In the end Leinster prevailed 19-15.

Don't fall short

Find out how we can help you at

LV.com

If you love it, LV= it

newcomers Dundee HSFP, Stirling County and Gala, all of whom had to acknowledge the supremacy for a second season of Melrose.

Gala's success in their first season back in the top tier was spectacular, culminating in the Netherdale club's cup final win over Ayr. Under the guidance of former Scotland and Borders assistant coach George Graham, Gala at one stage threatened to win the league, only to falter after the Christmas break before fighting back to finish in third position. Graham's tough coaching regime has transformed Gala and allowed young talents such as stand-off Lee Millar and winger Craig Robertson to flourish in what is de facto a professional environment.

But it was Gala's neighbours, Melrose, who again took the honours in the Premiership, the Greenyards side, coached by Craig Chalmers, playing a brand of rugby that made success inevitable. Central to their league victory was the durability of their veteran Scotland player Cammie Murray, whose sharpness in both attack and defence was key in a number of close games.

It looked in recent years as though club rugby was becoming dangerously concentrated in Edinburgh. The rise of Dundee HSFP, who finished second in the league, and Aberdeen, however, has provided a much healthier geographical spread in Scotland, and with Stirling County finishing fourth there is further proof that rugby outside the central belt is strong.

The capital still has four clubs in the Premiership – Heriot's, Boroughmuir, Currie and Edinburgh Accies – but for how much longer this is sustainable remains to be seen. Disappointingly, in terms of diversity, Glasgow Hawks failed to qualify for the top ten, as did that one-time powerhouse of Scottish rugby, Hawick.

The gap between the top end of the amateur game and the professional clubs in Scotland is slowly narrowing, and if this trend continues then the Premiership could act as a conduit to professional rugby for those later-developing players who have slipped through the age-grade filtering system. Indeed, it would become the interface between amateur and professional rugby, a fact that Murrayfield can ill afford to ignore.

BELOW Gala, winners of the RBS Cup, after defeating Ayr 24-10 in the final at Murrayfield. Gala also finished in third place in the RBS Premier A competition.

Wales: Farewell to Shane

by DAVID STEWART

'Shane Williams left us to a script that was surely heaven-sent: a try in his last appearance for Wales, one in his last game at the Liberty Stadium, and a brace in the Dublin final'

A year ago, this column ended with a sentence describing Wales as 'a proud (albeit not wealthy) rugby country'. A year on, the credit crunch has bitten in the regional rugby entities to the extent that pride – and smartness – will need to expand significantly to fill the wealth gap that has emerged. All four are learning to operate on reduced budgets, and with a salary cap, which has led to an outflow of expensive and high-profile players and coaches.

Come the autumn internationals, conceivably five of the national team's run-on XV will be playing their club football in France. With the departure of Nigel Davies to succeed Bryan Redpath at Gloucester, and of Scott Johnson to assist Andy Robinson in Scotland, all the Welsh teams have changed head coach in the last 18 months – an unprecedented rate of turnover. The promotions from within of Simon Easterby and Steve Tandy at the Scarlets and Ospreys respectively (as with Darren Edwards following Paul Turner the previous season) are illustrative of the financial issues; likewise the departures of Gethin Jenkins, Huw Bennett and Luke Charteris across the English Channel to join Mike Phillips, James Hook and Lee Byrne.

A review of the 2011-12 season suggests there is not much slack in the system. The Ospreys may have survived a turbulent mid-season interlude to end in outstanding fashion as RaboDirect

champions, but the Scarlets flattered before faltering, the Blues declined from promise to near meltdown, and the Dragons returned to toil and struggle.

Proudly, and properly so, the Ospreys sit atop the Celtic League arena once more. A close-run thing away in the last game that Aironi will play in the Rabo, when 14 men just held out in the last quarter for an 18-11 win and a home semi-final, was an unlikely precursor to the performance of the season. Munster were humbled 45-10, with Dan Biggar adding 25 points – in a 'coming-of-age' display – to the five tries scored by his colleagues in the Swansea sunshine. And so to the RDS to take on Leinster, who had retained their Heineken title a week earlier.

If the Ospreys directors had any doubts about the personnel changes they effected, the character their players showed on the last Sunday in May spoke volumes, turning a nine-point deficit with ten minutes left into a glorious 31-30 triumph. An injury-time corner try by the retiring Shane Williams, converted from the touch line by the ice-cool Biggar, was the sort of finale dreamed of by sponsors with a name nobody had previously heard of. The play-off win was an affirmation of Steve Tandy, who in his impressively understated manner said, 'Once we step onto the field, there's not too much talking, and we get on with the business.' Quite so.

A key element appears to be that men of character, who genuinely care for the region, remain at the core, notably the Jones boys: the estimable Ryan who enjoyed a rejuvenation to his best form;

ABOVE The Scarlets' England No. 8 Ben Morgan is chopped down at Northampton. The Welsh side won this Heineken Cup encounter 28-23.

FACING PAGE Shane Williams bows out with a try to give the Ospreys a chance of overhauling Leinster late in the RaboDirect final. Dan Biggar landed the winning conversion.

Alan-Wyn, the renewal of whose partnership with the long-term injured Ian Evans was vital; and the outstanding Adam, now a cult figure, but one possessed of a big heart and a sharp brain (and not just for rugby, much less the science of the scrum). The rapid progress of young talent was a joy to behold: Justin Tipuric, Rhys Webb and Ashley Beck will be major contributors in the era to come.

Scarlets will feel, rightly, that their level of performance and quality of play should have seen them join their rivals to the near east in the Rabo semi-finals. World Cup seasons are different, but a record of four defeats in their opening five league games (three to Irish provinces, also denuded by players in New Zealand) left them playing 'catch-up'. The chance to snatch fourth spot from Glasgow slipped away in a 26-23 defeat at Edinburgh at the end of March, and by the time of an exciting 20-20 draw with Munster at Parc y Scarlets in their penultimate fixture, it was clear their campaign would be an unfulfilled one. Still, their singular support will have enjoyed the modest consolation of a late-season 'double' over the Blues by 26-14 and 29-20.

Not only is Nigel Davies heading to the Forest of Dean but Ben Morgan (what a debt English rugby owes for the rapid development of the explosive young No. 8) has also returned to the land of his father. Lou Reed (no relation) moves to Cardiff, and the wonderful Stephen Jones is taking the M4 to Wasps, but Jonathan Davies heartened all by signing again; and with Rhys Priestland, Scott and Liam Williams, a fit-again Morgan Stoddart, and the titan that is George North round him, why wouldn't he? But will those forwards – led by another North Walian, Rob McCusker – produce enough ball?

The Heineken Cup has merited only the briefest mention in this narrative thus far. Scarlets started like a train, beating Castres at home in round one of the competition, then defeating Northampton away in round two, but a total of three wins out of six was never going to be enough; much less the two wins the Ospreys achieved. The Dragons having failed to make the starting gate, that left the Blues. Beaten by Edinburgh to the top of their (far from difficult) pool, they headed for Dublin and were put to the sword by the Irish champions in a 34-3 defeat that proved to be a defining afternoon. The Cardiff-based region won only one of their last six league games, including losses to all the other Welsh regions.

The blood-letting followed. The great Martyn Williams entered a well-deserved retirement; Ben Blair followed Jenkins to France, and other Kiwis moved on, too: Laulala to Munster; Tito and Rush to the pipe and slippers, although Xavier will assist new director of rugby Phil Davies in the role of

defence coach. The former Llanelli stalwart knows a culture change is needed. 'I plan to get every last drop of sweat, blood and enthusiasm out of the group.'

The Dragons have been the Cinderella team for longer now than they can be comfortable with. The outlook is not encouraged by a ninth-place finish being topped off with a year-end loss reported at £270,000, making a total debt owing of £2.3 million. Aled Brew may have joined Charteris in France, and Jason Tovey has moved the dozen or so miles from Newport to Cardiff, but happily Toby Faletau and the remarkable Dan Lydiate remain as rallying points. The premature retirement of hooker Lloyd Burns, due to a neck injury and damaged aorta, was an unwanted blow. (When we consider Rhys Thomas, a recent Dragon tight-head, retired from the Scarlets in April following a heart attack during training and subsequent emergency operation, one would hope the medical folk are paying close attention.)

Edwards strikes a note both realistic and determined: 'I knew this was going to be a season where we'd have to make a lot of changes. I'm expecting us to perform better next year. The development season is over. Fifteen players in the 2012-13 squad have come through the region's age group teams and semi-professional league.' Bold, too.

The only way this year's column can honourably end is in paying tribute to the outstanding talent that has been Shane Williams. The left wing left us to a script that was surely heaven-sent: a try against Australia in his last appearance for Wales at the Millennium Stadium, one in his last game at the Liberty Stadium (cheekily converted by himself) in a 31-12 hiding of the Dragons, and crucially the second of his brace in the Dublin final – all within moments of the final whistle.

No Welsh player since Gerald Davies has set the pulse of the entire rugby world racing in quite the same way as the little man from the Amman Valley – to where he will retire after a final, well-remunerated season in Japan. Those wishing to maintain their artistry ration at The Liberty may switch attention to the 'tiki-taka' entertainment of the round-ball game. Therein lies yet another threat to the financial health – via gate and merchandising receipts – and thus the rugby wellbeing of the Ospreys, and their neighbours and rivals.

FACING PAGE Blues' Martyn Williams is tackled by Leinster's Jonathan Sexton as the champions defeat Cardiff 34-3 in the Heineken Cup quarter-finals.

BELOW Martyn Thomas (15) and Pat Leach (12) get in the way of Aironi's Joshua Furno. The Dragons won this RaboDirect clash 23-14, but could manage only a ninth-place finish overall.

Wooden Spoon
The children's charity of rugby

www.woodenspoon.com

be part of our team

Text the word **SPOON** to **70300** and receive your Wooden Spoon wristband.

Your support will result in a £3.00 donation to Wooden Spoon for each text message you send.

Text messages cost £3, plus your standard network message charge (based on your service provider rates).

Winners
of the Spirit of Rugby
Award 2011

Wooden Spoon, 115-117 Fleet Road, Fleet, Hampshire, GU51 3PD, Charity Registration No 326691 (England & Wales) and SC039247 (Scotland)

Ireland: Leinster Clubs Hit the Top
by PETER O'REILLY

'There was some excitement yet to come, however, as Mary's still had to win their final game, at home to third-placed Young Munster. They came back from 16-3 behind'

Just as Leinster have established themselves as the dominant Irish province, winning three of the last four Heineken Cups, their clubs have begun to enjoy some success in the All Ireland League, now sponsored by Ulster Bank. In 2010-11, Old Belvedere broke a seven-year Munster hegemony by winning their first title, to be followed last season by St Mary's, claiming their first success since 2000. St Mary's and another Leinster club, Clontarf, proved to be the two best teams in 2011-12, and the only regret was they didn't get to go head-to-head on neutral territory. That was because last season, the clubs agreed to drop the play-off system at the end of the league programme – a pity, because this robbed them of a day at the Aviva Stadium in the full glare of the national media, which has shown decreasing interest in a competition that received a lot of coverage during its heyday in the 1990s.

BELOW Mark Sexton of St Mary's College goes over for the first of his two tries in his side's division 1A title-clinching victory over Young Munster in the last game of the season.

The system is up for review at the end of the 2012-13 season, when the clubs will again try to decide what is best for the league on a number of fronts. The problem with trying to get 52 clubs to come to some form of consensus is that there are such widely differing needs.

Currently, those clubs are broken into four divisions, with ten in 1A and 1B and 16 in 2A and 2B. The stronger clubs would naturally like to have more access to players on their books who are contracted to the provinces, whether in the academies or on the fringe of the RaboDirect PRO12 team. But as things stand, apparently for safety's sake, each side in divisions 1A and 1B is restricted to one forward and one back from the professional ranks. This seems a shame, given that so many young pros appear to spend more time in the gym than playing games, especially as the provincial 'A' team competition, the British & Irish Cup, has hardly set the world alight.

There appears to be general agreement that ten teams is the optimum for the top flight, and that this allows the clubs to keep some connection to the provinces. There's a demographic problem, however, given that 1A was made up only of clubs from Munster and Leinster last season – five each. That problem persists in this campaign, though with Munster now being represented by six clubs.

That is not to say a Munster champion is likely to emerge. Clubs from the southern province may have won 17 of the 22 titles in the league's history, with Limerick clubs winning 13 of those. For economic reasons, however, Limerick clubs in particular are struggling desperately to maintain standards – last year, nine-times champions Shannon only hung on to top-flight status by their fingernails. Players are leaving the city in search of work and it's in Dublin that work is most available – through contacts in the city's clubs.

The main chat in the build-up to last year's league was the exodus from Cork Con, four-times champions, to Clontarf – key players like Barry O'Mahony, Richie Lane and Frank Cogan. It was no secret that 'Tarf had facilitated this migration to the capital by providing jobs for players. Here was a club looking to use the economic downturn to their advantage. In certain quarters, the 'l' was even dropped from their club name, so that they became 'Con-tarf'. 'Tarf were the strongest team in the league for most of the season, and having lost three previous play-off finals, they surely felt their superiority would be made to count in a straight league format. But they failed to put any real daylight between themselves and the pack and when it came down to it, they blew the key game of the season. That was at home to Mary's on the penultimate Saturday, a game the visitors won 18-12 and also by three tries to two. No argument. There was some excitement yet to come, however, as Mary's still had to win their final game, at home to third-placed Young Munster. They came back from 16-3 behind, thanks to two final-quarter tries by Mark Sexton, brother to the Leinster and Ireland fly half.

At the other end of the table, Old Belvedere staged a most remarkable jailbreak, winning a series of games to nudge themselves off the

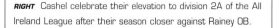
RIGHT Cashel celebrate their elevation to division 2A of the All Ireland League after their season closer against Rainey OB.

bottom of the table and above Blackrock, and then pipping promotion hopefuls Belfast Harlequins at Anglesea Road to win the play-off and secure their top-flight status for another year.

There they will be joined by UL Bohemian, who also finished the season at a ferocious gallop, playing bright, enterprising rugby under the guidance of their coach, Colm Tucker – son of the former Ireland and Lions flanker of the same name, who had sadly passed away earlier in the season. Beneath Bohs were four Ulster clubs – Belfast Harlequins, Dungannon, Ballynahinch and Ballymena – all of whom must try again to break up the Leinster/Munster cartel in 1A.

With them will be Dublin University, winners of 2A and keen to stay close to their arch-rivals, UCD, who just about survived in 1B. DU can only have been encouraged by the ease with which they topped their division, ending up 11 points clear of Malone, their nearest rivals.

Thomond, Instonians and Clonakilty all dropped to 2B, and spotted Cashel, Banbridge and Highfield passing them on the way up. If upwardly mobile Cashel were the success story of 2B, Wanderers were unfortunately the main talking point.

One of the founding members of the IRFU, and a favourite to win the inaugural All Ireland League in 1990-91, Wanderers have produced numerous Irish internationals over the years and five Ireland captains in total. They made a brave effort to retain senior status here, but not even a final-day one-point victory away to Banbridge could save them.

The word from Merrion Road in the close season was that serious efforts were being made to ensure that Wanderers' junior status was only a temporary condition. With Leinster proving so popular and successful at their RDS home less than half a mile away, the irony of Wanderers' plight is lost on no one.

next

We are proud to support
Wooden Spoon Rugby World

www.next.co.uk

France: Saint-André Takes the Wheel by CHRIS THAU

'The World Cup saw the end of Lièvremont's tenure as French coach, with former French winger and Gloucester, Sale and Toulon coach Philippe Saint-André taking over'

This was a mixed season for French rugby, defined somehow by a peculiar RWC campaign in New Zealand where the French team did not exactly cover themselves with glory, though they managed to reach the final, giving an unusually subdued All Blacks team a real fight. The French, blowing hot and cold, were not even supposed to reach the knockout stages, having lost in their pool to both New Zealand and Tonga – the latter result described as the biggest upset in RWC history – after an unimpressive win against Japan. It was another upset in their pool, with Canada defeating Tonga 25-20 in Whangarei, that secured France a quarter-final berth against an equally out-of-sorts England. Their display in that match was their most coherent performance, and was followed by their lamentable 9-8 win over 14-man Wales, in a match more memorable for Welsh gallantry than any French nous or enterprise. All these results came amid talk of disharmony in the French camp, as reports of conflicts between players and coach Mark Lièvremont percolated through the pages of the media.

It all exploded after the Welsh match, when the French players decided to go to town to celebrate, despite Lièvremont's warning that this could undermine their quest for the Webb Ellis Cup. The coach knew well enough what happens when French players let their hair down to celebrate a win. He was one of those who went to town in the aftermath of France's epic 1999 RWC semi-final win over the All Blacks at Twickenham, and the team paid the price a week later when they

BELOW In the hot seat. New France coach Philippe Saint-André before the second Test against Argentina, Tucumán, June 2012.

were thoroughly demolished 35-12 by the rampant Wallabies. The 'spoiled brats', as Lièvremont described his 2011 charges, refused to heed his request, and France failed again at the last hurdle. Did the beers washed down in downtown Auckland play a part in the subsequent French defeat? This is a factor difficult to quantify, though the conventional wisdom says that it might well have.

It is notoriously difficult to manage French players nurtured in the militant trade unionism of their parents and grandparents, while fuelled by the kind of demolition journalism practised by the country's leading sports newspaper *L'Equipe*. World Cups offer such opportunities, and not only in rugby, and *L'Equipe* grabs them with both hands. The vitriolic media campaign against France's soccer coach Aimé Jacquet in 1998 and the players' mutiny in South Africa which undermined coach Raymond Domenech in 2010 are still vivid in the memory. One wondered what would have been the verdict on Lièvremont had France managed to beat New Zealand in the final. The fact that Lièvremont was so outspoken in calling players 'undisciplined, disobedient and selfish' and even 'cowards' must give an idea about his personal turmoil when confronted with the unholy alliance between the chattering classes and his players, more concerned with pay cheques and contracts than the job in hand.

The World Cup saw the end of Lièvremont's tenure as French coach, with former French winger and Gloucester, Sale and Toulon coach Philippe Saint-André taking over. During his coaching stint in England with Gloucester and Sale, Saint-André, a phenomenally effective yet understated player with 69 French caps under his belt, had added a disciplinarian streak to his rigorous frame of mind. According to Kingsley Jones – his former coaching partner at both Gloucester and Sale, now coaching Russia – Saint-André is the 'best person in the world to be the French boss'. Consistency at the very top is what he aims for, though France in his first season in charge failed to acquire that elusive quality. Whether he will achieve his objective depends on many factors, of which the players, some of whom had been described in unflattering terms by Lièvremont, form the main category.

France won two and drew one of their five Six Nations matches, though their display in the 16-9 defeat by Wales at the end of the tournament might have been reasonably close to what Saint-André has in mind. Furthermore, in his search for new talent and with several of the regulars – Dusautoir, Yachvili, Harinordoquy and co. – allowed to rest or, in Servat's case, retired, his travelling squad to Argentina included no less than nine players who had never played for France before. Thanks to a late Argentine try, France lost the first Test 23-20 in Cordoba, but they redeemed themselves with a classy 49-10 demolition of the Pumas in the second Test. This was the kind of rugby Saint-André had been asking for, and France delivered in style. Whether they will be able to play like that consistently is another question.

In his search for consistency, Saint-André has asked two consummate artisans of French coaching to join his management team – Biarritz's Patrice Lagisquet as the backs coach and

Toulouse's Yannick Bru as the man in charge of the forwards. Unlike Lagisquet who joined Saint-André at the beginning of the year, Bru, a 39-year-old former international hooker, had to delay his arrival until his contract with Toulouse had run out at the end of the season. He joined Saint-André's coaching staff just before the tour to Argentina, and according to reports, one of the differences between the inadequate French effort in the first Test and the brilliance of the second was his relentless work with the forwards, not to mention Lagisquet's creativity and vision.

Bru, identified by Stade Toulousain head coach Guy Novès as one of the central factors in the club's dominance of the French domestic scene, was without doubt one of the masterminds of the nineteenth Toulouse success in the 113-year history of the French Championship. With Toulouse legend William Servat playing his last match for the club in the clash for the Bouclier de Brennus, it was the manner in which Toulouse destroyed Toulon's scrummage that gave a hint of Bru's role in an immeasurably satisfying win. Yes, it was ugly. Yes, they did not score tries. Yes, they defended more than they attacked. Yes, there was precious little of what we call French flair. But it was hard and uncompromising, and it was effective. Twelve of the 18 points scored by Luke McAlister in his kicking masterclass were the product of penalties awarded against the failing Toulon scrummage, with their tight-head Davit Kubriashvili earning a yellow card under the relentless battering of his Toulouse counterpart, the former Springbok loose-head Gurthrö Steenkamp.

At the other end of the spectrum, the man Toulon had expected to produce miracles once again, the one and only Jonny Wilkinson, failed with two of his kicks at goal – exactly the difference between winning and losing this strangely absorbing encounter. The local newspaper *Midi Olympique* called Stade Toulousain 'The Insatiables', a hint at their unrelenting pursuit of excellence and trophies, pointing out that Guy Novès had been involved in 12 of the club's 19 successful championship finals, two as a player and ten as coach. A remarkable record indeed.

FACING PAGE Wing Benjamin Fall after touching down for France in the 49-10 second Test win against Argentina in June 2012.

BELOW Census Johnston of Stade Toulousain is clattered to the ground during the French Championship final. In the scrummage set-piece it was all Toulouse, however, and Toulon paid with a string of penalties converted by Luke McAlister.

Italy: Dondi Steps Down; Calvisano Double Up

by CHRIS THAU

'Last year Dondi convinced Jacques Brunel to come to Rome, and under him the Italian team gained further in confidence, in quality of play and significantly in results'

The decision of the long-serving Italian Rugby Federation (FIR) president Giancarlo Dondi to step down after 16 years at the helm brings a most remarkable period in the modern history of Italian rugby to an end. Arguably the greatest achievement of the 77-year-old former Parma and Fiamme Oro lock forward has been the admission of Italy into the Six Nations, though his tenacious battle to make Italian rugby competitive at top international level is not too far behind in significance. Last year Dondi convinced the highly rated French coach Jacques Brunel to come to Rome, and under him the Italian team gained further in confidence, in quality of play and significantly in results. This was reflected in a generally superior Six Nations campaign, with Italy bagging another Scottish scalp and coming tantalisingly close to defeating Ireland. The fourth parameter of high performance, consistency, is still eluding Italy, and this is an area targeted by Brunel and his coaching staff.

BELOW Giancarlo Dondi (right), then still in office as president of the Italian Rugby Federation (FIR), with Jacques Brunel as the latter is introduced as Italy's new national coach.

The outcome of the summer tour to Argentina, Canada and the USA was merely satisfactory, with two wins (25-16 v Canada and 30-10 v USA) and one defeat (37-22 v Argentina), underlining one of the perennial problems of the Italian professional game, the lack of strength in depth. In this respect there is good and bad news for Brunel's long-term plans. The bad news is that Italy Under 20 failed in their planned objective of staying in the elite section of the Junior World Championship and were relegated again to the second division, the Junior World Trophy, after only one year.

The good news for the Frenchman is that a new Italian selection, Italia Emergenti (Emerging Italy), who take over from Italy A as Italy's 'Next Senior National Representative Team', saw action in the IRB Nations Cup in Bucharest in June. This new title is not just a linguistic exercise; it underlines a change of priorities at the top of the Italian game, too dependent on foreign imports, mainly from South Africa and Argentina, to keep the elite section of the game operational. The new representative team, coached by Gianluca Guidi and Stefano Romagnoli, was the youngest team in Bucharest but displayed the abundance of talent and quality that will certainly whet Brunel's appetite. Emerging Italy, the majority in their early twenties, complemented beautifully the uncapped contingent of seven in Brunel's touring squad to the Americas.

For next season, the now-defunct Aironi have been replaced by a new selection called Zebre (Zebras), who will be staffed and funded entirely by the Italian Federation. The team will be based in Parma and play home games at Parma's XXV Aprile Stadium. Roberto Manghi is the director of rugby, with Frenchman Christian Gajan as technical director and Italy's Vincenzo Troiani and Alessandro Troncon as coaches. Another former Italian international player, Fabio Ongaro, is the team manager.

Virtually the entire playing personnel of Aironi have been retained by Zebre, with 33 of the 36 players on the roster qualified to play for Italy. In addition to the 19 former Aironi players, there are 17 new recruits from Italian clubs, significantly not only from the traditional strongholds of Treviso, Rovigo and Padova but also from other clubs like Fiamme Oro, Crociati, Lazio and I Cavalieri Prato, which is good news indeed.

With two franchises, Treviso and Zebre, in the RaboDirect PRO12 and Heineken Cup, the Italian entries in the Challenge Cup are provided by the top four finishers in the Italian league, the newly named Campionato d'Eccellenza, formerly the Super 10. Calvisano, who merged with Amatori Milano in 1992, marked their return to the top flight of the domestic league in some style after two seasons in Serie A following voluntary relegation for financial reasons. At the other end of the table, San Gregorio of Catania dropped to the lower division.

In May 2012 the name of the ground where Calvisano play their matches changed from Stadio San Michele to Peroni Stadium, following the acquisition by the famous Italian beer brand of the sponsorship rights for the venue. It brought the club luck, as Calvisano managed to beat arch-rivals Rovigo 16-9 in the home round of their two-leg semi-final to advance to the Italian league final by one point on aggregate, having lost 14-8 at Rovigo at the end of April. I Cavalieri Prato reached the final in less traumatic circumstances, winning both legs of their semi-final against Mogliano (29-24 at Mogliano and 18-16 at home). All four semi-finalists – Calvisano, Cavalieri, Mogliano and Rovigo – will play in the 2012-13 European Challenge Cup.

In the first round of the final – also played over two legs, home and away – Calvisano managed to overcome a 14-point half-time Cavalieri lead in Prato to win 27-22, thanks to their dominant scrum, which earned them two penalty tries, awarded by referee Carlo Damasco in the 65th and 78th minutes. Cavalieri scored two tries through Billy Ngawini and Uili Kolo'ofai either side of the interval, with Rima Wakarua landing four penalties, while Calvisano added a further try through wing Alberto Bergamo, skipper Paul Griffen converting all three tries and landing two penalties.

In the second leg, a try by Tongan international Paino Hehea and 11 points from the boot of Griffen saw Calvisano through 16-14 (43-36 on aggregate) to a third national championship trophy, having also won in 2005 and 2007. Cavalieri, nevertheless, had fought back gallantly, with Riccardo Bocchino landing three penalties and Emanuele Leonardi going over for a try in the dying seconds of the game. However, it was too little too late. To round off a most satisfying season, Calvisano – who are coached by Andrea Cavinato, definitely one of the most gifted of the young Italian coaches – defeated Rome's leading club Lazio, 30-23, in the final of the Trofeo Eccellenza (formerly the Coppa Italia) at Prato to accomplish the coveted double.

A Summary of the Season 2011-12

by TERRY COOPER

RUGBY WORLD CUP 2011

POOL A

New Zealand	41	Tonga	10
France	47	Japan	21
Tonga	20	Canada	25
New Zealand	83	Japan	7
France	46	Canada	19
Tonga	31	Japan	18
New Zealand	37	France	17
Canada	23	Japan	23
France	14	Tonga	19
New Zealand	79	Canada	15

	P	W	D	L	F	A	BP	Pts
New Zealand	4	4	0	0	240	49	4	20
France	4	2	0	2	124	96	3	11
Tonga	4	2	0	2	80	98	1	9
Canada	4	1	1	2	82	168	0	6
Japan	4	0	1	3	69	184	0	2

POOL B

Scotland	34	Romania	24
Argentina	9	England	13
Scotland	15	Georgia	6
Argentina	43	Romania	8
England	41	Georgia	10
England	67	Romania	3
Argentina	13	Scotland	12
Georgia	25	Romania	9
England	16	Scotland	12
Argentina	25	Georgia	7

	P	W	D	L	F	A	BP	Pts
England	4	4	0	0	137	34	2	18
Argentina	4	3	0	1	90	40	2	14
Scotland	4	2	0	2	73	59	3	11
Georgia	4	1	0	3	48	90	0	4
Romania	4	0	0	4	44	169	0	0

POOL C

Australia	32	Italy	6
Ireland	22	USA	10
Russia	6	USA	13
Australia	6	Ireland	15
Italy	53	Russia	17
Australia	67	USA	5
Ireland	62	Russia	12
Italy	27	USA	10
Australia	68	Russia	22
Ireland	36	Italy	6

	P	W	D	L	F	A	BP	Pts
Ireland	4	4	0	0	135	34	1	17
Australia	4	3	0	1	173	48	3	15
Italy	4	2	0	2	92	95	2	10
USA	4	1	0	3	38	122	0	4
Russia	4	0	0	4	57	196	1	1

POOL D

Fiji	49	Namibia	25
South Africa	17	Wales	16
Samoa	49	Namibia	12
South Africa	49	Fiji	3
Wales	17	Samoa	10
South Africa	87	Namibia	0
Fiji	7	Samoa	27
Wales	81	Namibia	7
South Africa	13	Samoa	5
Wales	66	Fiji	0

	P	W	D	L	F	A	BP	Pts
South Africa	4	4	0	0	166	24	2	18
Wales	4	3	0	1	180	34	3	15
Samoa	4	2	0	2	91	49	2	10
Fiji	4	1	0	3	59	167	1	5
Namibia	4	0	0	4	44	266	0	0

KNOCKOUT STAGES

Quarter-finals

Ireland	10	Wales	22
England	12	France	19
South Africa	9	Australia	11
New Zealand	33	Argentina	10

Semi-finals

Wales	8	France	9
Australia	6	New Zealand	20

Third-place Play-off

Wales	18	Australia	21

Final

France	7	New Zealand	8

INTERNATIONAL RUGBY

ENGLAND TO SOUTH AFRICA, JUNE 2012

Opponents	Results
SOUTH AFRICA	L 17-22
SA Southern Barbarians	W 54-26
SOUTH AFRICA	L 27-36
SA Northern Barbarians	W 57-31
SOUTH AFRICA	D 14-14

Played 5 Won 2 Drawn 1 Lost 2

SCOTLAND TO AUSTRALIA & SOUTH PACIFIC, JUNE 2012

Opponents	Results
AUSTRALIA	W 9-6
FIJI	W 37-25
SAMOA	W 17-16

Played 3 Won 3

WALES TO AUSTRALIA, JUNE 2012

Opponents	Results
AUSTRALIA	L 19-27
ACT Brumbies	W 25-15
AUSTRALIA	L 23-25
AUSTRALIA	L 19-20

Played 4 Won 1 Lost 3

IRELAND TO NEW ZEALAND, JUNE 2012

Opponents	Results
NEW ZEALAND	L 10-42
NEW ZEALAND	L 19-22
NEW ZEALAND	L 0-60

Played 3 Lost 3

FRANCE TO ARGENTINA, JUNE 2012

Opponents	Results
ARGENTINA	L 20-23
ARGENTINA	W 49-10

Played 2 Won 1 Lost 1

ITALY TO ARGENTINA & NORTH AMERICA JUNE 2012

Opponents	Results
ARGENTINA	L 22-37
CANADA	W 25-16
USA	W 30-10

Played 3 Won 2 Lost 1

ROYAL BANK OF SCOTLAND 6 NATIONS CHAMPIONSHIP 2012

Results

France	30	Italy	12
Scotland	6	England	13
Ireland	21	Wales	23
Italy	15	England	19
Wales	27	Scotland	13
Ireland	42	Italy	10
England	12	Wales	19
Scotland	17	France	23
France	17	Ireland	17
Wales	24	Italy	3
Ireland	32	Scotland	14
France	22	England	24
Italy	13	Scotland	6
Wales	16	France	9
England	30	Ireland	9

Final Table

	P	W	D	L	F	A	PD	Pts
Wales	5	5	0	0	109	58	51	10
England	5	4	0	1	98	71	27	8
Ireland	5	2	1	2	121	94	27	5
France	5	2	1	2	101	86	15	5
Italy	5	1	0	4	53	121	-68	2
Scotland	5	0	0	5	56	108	-52	0

OTHER INTERNATIONAL MATCH 2011

Wales	18	Australia	24

WORLD CUP WARM-UP MATCHES 2011

England	23	Wales	19
Scotland	10	Ireland	6
Wales	19	England	9
France	19	Ireland	12
Italy	31	Japan	24
Wales	28	Argentina	13
Ireland	22	France	26
Scotland	23	Italy	12
Ireland	9	England	20

UNDER 20 SIX NATIONS 2012

Results

Ireland	11	Wales	6
Scotland	3	England	59
Wales	28	Scotland	15
France	12	Ireland	13
France	19	Italy	5
Ireland	27	Italy	8
Scotland	21	France	30
England	40	Wales	9
Italy	7	England	42
Ireland	26	Scotland	0
Wales	30	Italy	23
France	12	England	8
Italy	17	Scotland	20
Wales	16	France	36
England	20	Ireland	9

Final Table

	P	W	D	L	F	A	PD	Pts
England	5	4	0	1	169	40	129	8
France	5	4	0	1	109	63	46	8
Ireland	5	4	0	1	86	46	40	8
Wales	5	2	0	3	89	125	-36	4
Scotland	5	1	0	4	59	160	-101	2
Italy	5	0	0	5	60	138	-78	0

CRAFTED

FOR THE

MOMENT

SINCE 1799

GREENE KING
BURY ST EDMUNDS

IPA

HANDCRAFTED INDIA PALE ALE

greenekingipa.co.uk

IRB PACIFIC NATIONS CUP 2012

(Held in June in Japan)

Samoa	20	Tonga	18
Fiji	25	Japan	19
Fiji	26	Samoa	29
Japan	20	Tonga	24
Samoa	27	Japan	26
Tonga	17	Fiji	29

Champions: Samoa

IRB NATIONS CUP 2012

(Held in June in Bucharest, Romania)

Romania	29	Uruguay	9
Russia	17	Emerging Italy	33
Portugal	9	Argentina Jaguars	41
Portugal	21	Emerging Italy	28
Romania	23	Argentina Jaguars	21
Russia	19	Uruguay	13
Russia	9	Argentina Jaguars	33
Portugal	7	Uruguay	35
Romania	17	Emerging Italy	13

Champions: Romania

IRB JUNIOR WORLD CHAMPIONSHIP 2012

(Held in June in South Africa)

Semi-finals

New Zealand	30	Wales	6
South Africa	35	Argentina	3

Final

South Africa	22	New Zealand	16

IRB JUNIOR WORLD RUGBY TROPHY 2012

(Held in June in Utah, USA)

Final

USA	37	Japan	33

FIRA/AER EUROPEAN UNDER 18 CHAMPIONSHIP 2012 – ELITE DIVISION

(Held in March/April in Madrid, Spain)

Quarter-finals

England	58	Georgia	8
Ireland	34	Portugal	24
Wales	41	Italy	8
France	19	Scotland	7

Fifth-place Final

Scotland	29	Georgia	10

Seventh-place Final

Portugal	14	Italy	41

Semi-finals

England	22	Wales	16
Ireland	22	France	20

Third-place Final

France	10	Wales	7

Final

Ireland	13	England	25

TRI-NATIONS 2011

Results

Australia	39	South Africa	20
New Zealand	40	South Africa	7
New Zealand	30	Australia	14
South Africa	9	Australia	14
South Africa	18	New Zealand	5
Australia	25	New Zealand	20

Champions: Australia

Note: From 2012 the Tri-Nations will be replaced by a four nations tournament, to include Argentina.

HSBC SEVENS WORLD SERIES FINALS 2011-12

Australia (Gold Coast)

New Zealand	12	Fiji	26

Dubai

England	29	France	12

South Africa (Port Elizabeth)

South Africa	26	New Zealand	31

New Zealand (Wellington)

New Zealand	24	Fiji	7

USA (Las Vegas)

New Zealand	19	Samoa	26

Hong Kong

Fiji	35	New Zealand	28

Japan (Tokyo)

Australia	28	Samoa	26

Scotland (Glasgow)

England	14	New Zealand	29

England (Twickenham)

Fiji	38	Samoa	15

Champions: New Zealand

WOMEN'S SIX NATIONS 2012

Results

France	32	Italy	0
Scotland	0	England	47
France	8	Ireland	7
Wales	20	Scotland	0
Italy	3	England	43
Ireland	40	Italy	10
Scotland	0	France	23
England	33	Wales	0
Ireland	36	Wales	0
Ireland	20	Scotland	0
Wales	30	Italy	13
France	3	England	15
England	23	Ireland	6
Italy	29	Scotland	12
Wales	0	France	31

Final Table

	P	W	D	L	F	A	PD	Pts
England	5	5	0	0	161	12	149	10
France	5	4	0	1	97	22	75	8
Ireland	5	3	0	2	109	41	68	6
Wales	5	2	0	3	50	113	-63	4
Italy	5	1	0	4	55	157	-102	2
Scotland	5	0	0	5	12	139	-127	0

CLUB, COUNTY AND DIVISIONAL RUGBY

ENGLAND

Aviva Premiership

	P	W	D	L	F	A	BP	Pts
Harlequins	22	17	1	4	526	389	5	75
Leicester	22	15	1	6	647	475	12	74
Saracens	22	16	1	5	489	350	7	73
Northampton	22	14	0	8	539	374	9	65
Exeter	22	12	0	10	436	421	11	59
Sale	22	10	0	12	453	538	9	49
London Irish	22	8	1	13	514	516	12	46
Bath	22	9	0	13	365	412	8	44
Gloucester	22	8	1	13	456	507	10	44
Worcester	22	7	1	14	322	448	6	36
Wasps	22	6	0	16	363	502	9	33
Newcastle	22	6	2	14	351	529	4	32

Relegated: Newcastle

Aviva Premiership Play-offs

Semi-finals

Harlequins	25	Northampton	23
Leicester	24	Saracens	15

Final

Harlequins	30	Leicester	23

RFUW Premiership Champions: Richmond

RFU National Championship
Play-Off Winners: London Welsh
Play-Off Runners-up: Cornish Pirates

Promoted to Premiership: London Welsh

National Leagues
National 1 Champions: Jersey
Runners-up: Ealing Trailfinders
National 2 (S) Champions: Old Albanians
Runners-up: Richmond
National 2 (N) Champions: Loughborough Students
Runners-up: Caldy

National 2 N & S Runners-up Play-off

Richmond	20	Caldy	13

RFU Knockout Trophy Finals

Intermediate Cup

East Grinstead	34	Ilkley	18

Senior Vase

Wath upon Dearne	22	Wells	31

Junior Vase

Harrow	3	Baildon	6

County Championships

Bill Beaumont Cup Division One Final

Hertfordshire	38	Lancashire	20

Division Two (S) Champions: Kent
Division Two (N) Champions: Durham

County Championship Shield Final

Surrey	43	Leicestershire	12

National Under 20 Championship Final

Gloucestershire	22	Yorkshire	28

Oxbridge University Matches

Varsity Match

Oxford	28	Cambridge	10

Under 21 Varsity Match

Oxford	19	Cambridge	11

Women's Varsity Match

Oxford	28	Cambridge	8

BUCS Competitions
Men's Championship Winners: UWE Hartpury
Women's C'ship Winners: UWIC

Inter-Service Championship

Army	59	RAF	0
Royal Navy	13	RAF	6
Army	48	Royal Navy	9

Champions: Army

Hospitals Cup Winners: Barts and The London

Middlesex Sevens 2011
Men's Champions: ULR Samurai International
Women's Champions: Wooden Spoon Women

Rosslyn Park Schools Sevens
Open Winners: Coleg Sir Gar
Festival Winners: Wellington College
Colts Winners: St Joseph's College
Preparatory Winners: Bishop's Stortford College
Juniors Winners: St Benedict's School
Girls Winners: Moulton College

Daily Mail Schools Day
Under 18 Cup Winners: Dulwich College
Under 18 Vase Winners: The Leys School
Under 15 Cup Winners: GS at Leeds
Under 15 Vase Winners: Dauntsey's School

SCOTLAND

RBS Cup
Semi-finals

Dundee HSFP	19	Gala	26
Ayr	30	Boroughmuir	25

Final

Gala	24	Ayr	10

RBS Shield Final

Dunfermline	11	Musselburgh	9

RBS Bowl Final

Dunbar	7	Helensburgh	13

Scottish Sevens Winners
Kelso: Watsonians
Selkirk: Watsonians
Melrose: Saracens
Hawick: Hawick
Berwick: Jed-Forest
Langholm: Hawick
Peebles: Watsonians
Gala: Jed-Forest
Earlston: Melrose
Jed-Forest: Heriot's
Kings of the Sevens: Jed-Forest

RBS Premier 1

	P	W	D	L	F	A	BP	Pts
Melrose	11	9	0	2	318	210	8	44
Gala	11	9	0	2	281	171	7	43
Dundee HSFP	11	8	0	3	301	235	6	38
Currie	11	7	0	4	369	219	7	35
Stirling County	11	6	1	4	271	246	5	31
Ayr	11	7	0	4	219	234	3	31
Aberdeen GS	11	6	0	5	256	230	5	29
Boroughmuir	11	4	0	7	268	245	8	24
Heriot's	11	3	0	8	194	266	4	16
Glasgow Hawks	11	3	1	7	160	308	1	15
Edinburgh Accies	11	2	1	8	196	333	4	14
Hawick	11	0	1	10	152	288	5	7

RBS Premier 2

	P	W	D	L	F	A	BP	Pts
Stewart's Melville	11	10	0	1	283	187	5	45
Watsonians	11	8	0	3	300	270	5	37
Jed-Forest	11	7	0	4	275	185	8	36
Hamilton	11	6	1	4	267	222	6	32
Selkirk	11	7	0	4	234	227	3	31
Kelso	11	5	0	6	237	252	5	25
Biggar	11	5	0	6	221	223	4	24
Falkirk	11	3	2	6	281	313	7	23
Hillhead/J'hill	11	3	0	8	239	260	10	22
Whitecraigs	11	4	0	7	163	215	4	20
West of Scotland	11	3	1	7	242	287	5	19
Peebles	11	3	0	8	174	275	4	16

RBS Premier 3
Champions: Howe of Fife
Runners-up: GHA

WALES

SWALEC Cup
Semi-finals

Cross Keys	19	Ebbw Vale	19
	(Cross Keys won on try count)		
Pontypridd	28	Newbridge	24

Final

Cross Keys	32	Pontypridd	19

SWALEC Plate Final

Penallta	21	Nant Conwy	15

SWALEC Bowl Final

Glyncoch	16	New Tredegar	14

Principality Premiership

	P	W	D	L	F	A	BP	Pts
Pontypridd	26	19	0	7	718	420	15	91
Llanelli	26	19	0	7	765	555	13	89
Aberavon	26	19	1	6	683	453	10	88
Llandovery	26	18	0	8	590	429	11	83
Neath	26	15	1	10	673	479	16	78
Cross Keys	26	15	0	11	629	566	13	73
Carmarthen	26	14	0	12	574	521	15	71
Bridgend	26	12	2	12	676	673	11	63
Cardiff Rugby	26	10	2	14	628	617	14	58
Swansea	26	9	1	16	574	675	13	51
Newport	26	9	0	17	568	735	11	47
Pontypool	26	9	1	16	503	639	9	47
Bedwas	26	9	0	17	521	652	5	41
Tonmawr	26	1	0	25	395	1083	6	10

SWALEC League Division 1 East

	P	W	D	L	F	A	BP	Pts
Ebbw Vale	22	19	0	3	793	215	19	95
Bargoed	22	18	0	4	610	299	14	86
Newbridge	22	18	0	4	559	265	11	83
Gilfach Goch	22	15	0	7	518	373	13	73
Beddau	22	12	0	10	410	453	7	55
Blackwood	22	9	0	13	347	424	9	45
Treorchy	22	9	1	12	355	430	7	45
The Wanderers	22	8	0	14	465	564	7	39
Merthyr	22	8	0	14	406	609	7	39
Rumney	22	7	2	13	414	561	7	39
Mountain Ash	22	6	1	15	322	483	6	32
Tredegar	22	1	0	21	252	775	5	9

SWALEC League Division 1 West

	P	W	D	L	F	A	BP	Pts
Corus	22	17	1	4	598	391	12	82
Narberth	22	17	0	5	623	440	13	81
Carmarthen Ath	22	14	0	8	478	359	11	67
Llangennech	22	13	0	9	455	434	8	60
Whitland	22	12	1	9	387	403	3	53
Bridgend Ath	22	9	1	12	461	455	13	51
UWIC	22	9	1	12	442	465	11	49
Llanharan	22	9	1	12	436	447	11	49
Tondu	22	9	0	13	444	460	11	47
Waunarlwydd	22	7	1	14	467	572	14	44
Bonymaen	22	8	0	14	373	472	8	40
Ammanford	22	4	2	16	349	615	11	31

IRELAND

Ulster Bank League Division 1A
	P	W	D	L	F	A	BP	Pts
St Mary's Coll	18	15	0	3	365	257	6	66
Clontarf	18	14	0	4	427	254	8	64
Young Munster	18	12	0	6	346	333	6	54
Cork Const'n	18	10	0	8	323	272	9	49
Lansdowne	18	9	0	9	450	370	12	48
Garryowen	18	8	1	9	337	331	11	45
Dolphin	18	6	0	12	304	376	9	33
Shannon	18	6	2	10	292	341	2	30
Old Belvedere	18	4	1	13	309	382	11	29
Blackrock Coll	18	4	0	14	266	503	8	24

Ulster Bank League Division 1B
	P	W	D	L	F	A	BP	Pts
UL Bohemian	18	12	0	6	348	252	9	57
Belfast H'quins	18	12	0	6	399	344	8	56
Dungannon	18	10	1	7	482	361	13	55
Ballynahinch	18	9	2	7	340	313	8	48
Ballymena	18	9	1	8	330	325	10	48
Buccaneers	18	10	0	8	332	329	9	47
Bruff	18	9	0	9	293	330	3	39
UCD	18	7	2	9	354	409	6	38
Galwegians	18	7	0	11	364	402	9	37
UCC	18	2	0	16	279	456	7	15

Ulster Bank League Division 2A
Champions: Dublin University

Ulster Bank League Division 2B
Champions: Cashel

All Ireland Provincial League Championship
Monivea	29	Richmond	20
Skerries	41	Clogher Valley	0
Clogher Valley	21	Monivea	20
Richmond	7	Skerries	19
Richmond	30	Clogher Valley	19
Skerries	27	Monivea	20

Champions: Skerries

All Ireland Cup Final
Garryowen	24	Ballymena	6

All Ireland Junior Cup Final
Tullamore	9	Monivea	3

All Ireland Under 21 Championship Final
Old Belvedere	11	UCD	17

RABODIRECT PRO12 2011-12

	P	W	D	L	F	A	BP	Pts
Leinster	22	18	1	3	568	326	7	81
Ospreys	22	16	1	5	491	337	5	71
Munster	22	14	1	7	489	367	9	67
Warriors	22	13	4	5	445	321	5	65
Scarlets	22	12	2	8	446	373	10	62
Ulster	22	12	0	10	474	424	8	56
Blues	22	10	0	12	446	460	10	50
Connacht	22	7	1	14	321	433	7	37
Dragons	22	7	1	14	370	474	6	36
Treviso	22	7	0	15	419	558	8	36
Edinburgh	22	6	1	15	454	588	6	32
Aironi	22	4	0	18	289	551	6	22

RaboDirect PRO12 Play-offs
Semi-finals
Ospreys	45	Munster	10
Leinster	19	Warriors	15

Final
Leinster	30	Ospreys	31

LV= CUP 2011-12

Semi-finals
Bath	16	Leicester	17
Northampton	27	Scarlets	12

Final
Leicester	26	Northampton	14

BRITISH & IRISH CUP 2011-12

Final
Munster A	31	Cross Keys	12

FRANCE

'Top 14' Play-offs

Semi-finals
Toulouse	24	Castres Olympique	15
Clermont Auvergne	12	Toulon	15

Final
Toulouse	18	Toulon	12

ITALY

Campionato d'Eccellenza

Final
I Cavalieri Prato   22   Calvisano   27
Calvisano   16   I Cavalieri Prato   14
(Calvisano win 43-36 on aggregate)

HEINEKEN CUP 2011-12

Quarter-finals
Saracens   3   Cl'mont Auvergne   22
Leinster   34   Blues   3
Edinburgh   19   Toulouse   14
Munster   16   Ulster   22

Semi-finals
Ulster   22   Edinburgh   19
Clermont Auvergne   15   Leinster   19

Final
Leinster   42   Ulster   14

AMLIN CHALLENGE CUP 2011-12

Quarter-finals
Wasps   23   Biarritz Olympique   26
Toulon   37   Harlequins   8
Stade Français   22   Exeter Chiefs   17
Brive   15   Scarlets   11

Semi-finals
Toulon   32   Stade Français   29
Biarritz Olympique   19   Brive   0

Final
Biarritz Olympique   21   Toulon   18

NEW ZEALAND

ITM Cup 2011

Final
Canterbury   12   Waikato   3

Heartland Championship 2011
Meads Cup: Wanganui
Lochore Cup: Poverty Bay

Ranfurly Shield holders: Taranaki

SOUTH AFRICA

Currie Cup 2011

Final
Sharks   16   Lions   42

SUPER RUGBY 2012

Final Table

	P	W	D	L	F	A	BP	Pts
Stormers	16	14	0	2	350	254	2	66
Chiefs	16	12	0	4	444	358	8	64
Reds	16	11	0	5	359	347	6	58
Crusaders	16	11	0	5	485	343	9	61
Bulls	16	10	0	6	472	369	11	59
Sharks	16	10	0	6	436	348	11	59
Brumbies	16	10	0	6	404	331	10	58
Hurricanes	16	10	0	6	489	429	9	57
Highlanders	16	9	0	7	359	385	6	50
Cheetahs	16	5	0	11	391	458	10	38
Waratahs	16	4	0	12	346	407	11	35
Blues	16	4	0	12	359	430	8	32
M'bourne Rebels	16	4	0	12	362	520	7	32
Western Force	16	3	0	13	306	440	7	27
Lions	16	3	0	13	317	460	5	25

Quarter-finals
Crusaders   28   Bulls   13
Reds   17   Sharks   30

Semi-finals
Chiefs   20   Crusaders   17
Stormers   19   Sharks   26

Final
Chiefs   37   Sharks   6

Key
Stormers: Conference winners
Crusaders: Wild Card teams

Note: The top two Conference winners – Stormers and Chiefs – received a bye in the quarter-finals.

BARBARIANS

Opponents	Results
South of Scotland	L 15-22
Australia	L 11-60
Loughborough Students	W 40-7
England	L 26-57
Ireland	W 29-28
Wales	L 21-30

Played 6 Won 2 Lost 4

PREVIEW OF THE
SEASON 2012-13

Key Players
selected by IAN ROBERTSON

ENGLAND

ALEX GOODE
Saracens
Born: 5 May 1988
Height: 5ft 11ins Weight: 14st 8lbs
Fly half/Full back – 2 caps
1st cap v South Africa 2012

CHRIS ROBSHAW
Harlequins
Born: 4 June 1986
Height: 6ft 2ins Weight: 17st 4lbs
Back-row – 8 caps
1st cap v Argentina 2009

SCOTLAND

GREIG LAIDLAW
Edinburgh Rugby
Born: 12 October 1985
Height: 5ft 9ins Weight: 12st 6lbs
Fly half/Scrum half – 10 caps
1st cap v New Zealand 2010

DAVID DENTON
Edinburgh Rugby
Born: 5 February 1990
Height: 6ft 5ins Weight: 17st 11lbs
Back-row – 6 caps
1st cap v Ireland 2011

WALES

RHYS PRIESTLAND
Scarlets
Born: 9 January 1987
Height: 6ft Weight: 14st 13lbs
Fly half – 18 caps
1st cap v Scotland 2011

DAN LYDIATE
Dragons
Born: 18 December 1987
Height: 6ft 4ins Weight: 18st 2lbs
Back-row – 27 caps
1st cap v Argentina 2009

Six Nations Championship

2012-13

IRELAND

CONOR MURRAY
Munster
Born: 20 April 1989
Height: 6ft 2ins Weight: 14st 10lbs
Scrum half – 12 caps
1st cap v France 2011

SEAN O'BRIEN
Leinster
Born: 14 February 1987
Height: 6ft 2ins Weight: 16st 13lbs
Back-row – 22 caps
1st cap v Fiji 2009

FRANCE

MAXIME MERMOZ
Toulon
Born: 28 July 1986
Height: 5ft 11ins Weight: 14st 9lbs
Centre – 19 caps
1st cap v Australia 2008

LOUIS PICAMOLES
Toulouse
Born: 5 February 1986
Height: 6ft 4ins Weight: 16st 10lbs
Back-row – 28 caps
1st cap v Ireland 2008

ITALY

KRIS BURTON
Treviso
Born: 4 August 1980
Height: 5ft 11ins Weight: 13st 10lbs
Fly half – 17 caps
1st cap v Uruguay 2007

ALESSANDRO ZANNI
Treviso
Born: 31 January 1984
Height: 6ft 4ins Weight: 17st
Back-row – 66 caps
1st cap v Tonga 2005

Fixtures 2012-13

AUGUST 2012

Sat. 18th	AUSTRALIA v NZ (RC)
	SA v ARGENTINA (RC)
Sat. 25th	NZ v AUSTRALIA (RC)
	ARGENTINA v SA (RC)
	RBS Scottish Premier League
	RBS Scottish National League
	RBS Scottish Ch/ship A & B
Fri. 31st to	
Sun. 2nd Sept	RaboDirect PRO12 (1)
	English National Championship

SEPTEMBER 2012

Sat. 1st	English National Leagues
	RBS Scottish Premier League
	RBS Scottish National League
	RBS Scottish Ch/ship A & B
	Welsh Principality Premiership
	Swalec pan-Wales Nat Ch/ship
	Swalec Welsh National Lges
Sat. 1st and	
Sun. 2nd	Aviva English Premiership (1)
Fri. 7th to	
Sun. 9th	Aviva English Premiership (2)
	RaboDirect PRO12 (2)
	English National Championship
Sat. 8th	AUSTRALIA v SA (RC)
	NZ v ARGENTINA (RC)
	English National Leagues
	RBS Scottish Premier League
	RBS Scottish National League
	RBS Scottish Ch/ship A & B
	Welsh Principality Premiership
	Swalec pan-Wales Nat Ch/ship
	Swalec Welsh National Lges
Fri. 14th to	
Sun. 16th	Aviva English Premiership (3)
	RaboDirect PRO12 (3)
	English National Championship
Sat. 15th	AUSTRALIA v ARGENTINA (RC)
	NZ v SA (RC)
	English National Leagues
	RBS Scottish Premier League
	RBS Scottish National League
	RBS Scottish Ch/ship A & B
	Welsh Principality Premiership
	Swalec pan-Wales Nat Ch/ship
	Swalec Welsh National Lges
Wed. 19th	Welsh Principality Premiership
Fri. 21st to	
Sun. 23rd	Aviva English Premiership (4)
	RaboDirect PRO12 (4)
Sat. 22nd	English National Leagues
	RBS Scottish Premier League
	RBS Scottish National League
	RBS Scottish Ch/ship A & B
	Welsh Principality Premiership

	Swalec pan-Wales Nat Ch/ship
	Swalec Welsh National Lges
Sat. 22nd and	
Sun. 23rd	English National Championship
Fri. 28th and	
Sat 29th	English National Championship
	UB Irish Leagues 1A/B, 2A/B
Fri. 28th to	
Sun. 30th	Aviva English Premiership (5)
	RaboDirect PRO12 (5)
Sat. 29th	SA v AUSTRALIA (RC)
	ARGENTINA v NZ (RC)
	English National Leagues
	RBS Scottish Premier League
	RBS Scottish National League
	RBS Scottish Ch/ship A & B
	Welsh Principality Premiership
	Swalec pan-Wales Nat Ch/ship
	Swalec Welsh National Lges

OCTOBER 2012

Fri. 5th and	
Sat. 6th	English National Championship
	UB Irish Leagues 1A/B, 2A/B
Fri. 5th to	
Sun. 7th	Aviva English Premiership (6)
	RaboDirect PRO12 (6)
Sat. 6th	SA v NZ (RC)
	English National Leagues
	RBS Scottish Premier League
	RBS Scottish National League
	RBS Scottish Ch/ship A & B
	Welsh Principality Premiership
	Swalec pan-Wales Nat Ch/ship
	Swalec Welsh National Lges
Sun. 7th	ARGENTINA v AUSTRALIA (RC)
Thu. 11th to	
Sun. 14th	Heineken Cup (1)
	Amlin Challenge Cup (1)
Fri. 12th and	
Sat. 13th	UB Irish League 2B
Fri. 12th to	
Sun. 14th	British & Irish Cup (1)
Sat. 13th	English National Leagues
	RBS Scottish Premier League
	RBS Scottish National League
	RBS Scottish Ch/ship A & B
	Swalec pan-Wales Nat Ch/ship
	Swalec Welsh National Lges
Thu. 18th to	
Sun. 21st	Heineken Cup (2)
	Amlin Challenge Cup (2)
Fri. 19th to	
Sun. 21st	British & Irish Cup (2)
Sat. 20th	English National Leagues
	RBS Scottish Premier League
	RBS Scottish National League

RBS Scottish Ch/ship A & B
Swalec pan-Wales Nat Ch/ship
Swalec Welsh National Lges

Fri. 26th and
Sat. 27th   UB Irish Leagues 1A/B, 2A/B
Fri. 26th to
Sun. 28th   Aviva English Premiership (7)
             RaboDirect PRO12 (7)
             English National Championship
Sat. 27th   English National Leagues
             RBS Scottish Premier League
             RBS Scottish National League
             RBS Scottish Ch/ship A & B
             Welsh Principality Premiership
             Swalec pan-Wales Nat Ch/ship
             Swalec Welsh National Lges

NOVEMBER 2012

Fri. 2nd and
Sat. 3rd   UB Irish Leagues 1A/B, 2A/B
Fri. 2nd to
Sun. 4th   Aviva English Premiership (8)
             RaboDirect PRO12 (8)
Sat. 3rd   English National Leagues
             RBS Scottish Premier League
             RBS Scottish National League
             RBS Scottish Ch/ship A & B
             Welsh Principality Premiership
             Swalec pan-Wales Nat Ch/ship
             Swalec Welsh National Lges
Sat. 3rd and
Sun. 4th   English National Championship
Fri. 9th to
Sun. 11th   English National Championship
Sat. 10th   ENGLAND v FIJI
             IRELAND v SA
             SCOTLAND v NZ
             WALES v ARGENTINA
             LV= (Anglo-Welsh) Cup (1)
             English National Leagues 1/2
Fri. 16th   WALES v SAMOA
Fri. 16th and
Sat. 17th   English National Leagues
Sat. 17th   ENGLAND v AUSTRALIA
             IRELAND v FIJI
             SCOTLAND v SA
             LV= (Anglo-Welsh) Cup (2)
             Welsh Principality Premiership
             Swalec pan-Wales Nat Ch/ship
             Swalec Welsh National Lges
             UB Irish Leagues 1A/B, 2A/B
Fri. 23rd to
Sun. 25th   Aviva English Premiership (9)
             RaboDirect PRO12 (9)
             English National Championship
             Welsh Principality Premiership
Sat. 24th   ENGLAND v SA
             IRELAND v ARGENTINA
             SCOTLAND v TONGA
             WALES v NZ
             English National Leagues

Wed. 28th   Swalec pan-Wales Nat Ch/ship
Fri. 30th to
Sat. 1st Dec UB Irish Leagues 1A/B, 2A/B
Fri. 30th to
Sun. 2nd Dec Aviva English Premiership (10)
             RaboDirect PRO12 (10)
             English National Championship
             Welsh Principality Premiership

DECEMBER 2012

Sat. 1st   ENGLAND v NZ
             WALES v AUSTRALIA
             RBS Scottish Premier League
             RBS Scottish National League
             RBS Scottish Ch/ship A & B
Thu. 6th   Oxford U v Cambridge U
                 (Twickenham)
Thu. 6th to
Sun. 9th   Heineken Cup (3)
             Amlin Challenge Cup (3)
Fri. 7th and
Sat. 8th   UB Irish Leagues 2A/B
Fri. 7th to
Sun. 9th   British & Irish Cup (3)
Sat. 8th   English National Leagues
             Swalec pan-Wales Nat Ch/ship
             Swalec Welsh National Lges
Thu. 13th to
Sun. 16th   Heineken Cup (4)
             Amlin Challenge Cup (4)
Fri. 14th to
Sun. 16th   British & Irish Cup (4)
Sat. 15th   English National Leagues
             UB Irish League 2A
Fri. 21st to
Sun. 23rd   Aviva English Premiership (11)
             RaboDirect PRO12 (11)
Sat. 22nd   English National Leagues 1/2
             RBS Scottish Premier League
             RBS Scottish National League
             RBS Scottish Ch/ship A & B
             Welsh Principality Premiership
             Swalec pan-Wales Nat Ch/ship
             Swalec Welsh National Lges
Sat. 22nd and
Sun. 23rd   English National Championship
Wed. 26th   English National Championship
Wed. 26th and
Thu. 27th   Welsh Principality Premiership
Fri. 28th to
Sun. 30th   Aviva English Premiership (12)
             RaboDirect PRO12 (12)
Sat. 29th   Swalec pan-Wales Nat Ch/ship
             Swalec Welsh National Lges

JANUARY 2013

Tue. 1st   English National Championship
Fri. 4th and
Sat. 5th   UB Irish Leagues 1A/B
Fri. 4th to
Sun. 6th   Aviva English Premiership (13)

Sat. 5th	RaboDirect PRO12 (13)
	English National Championship
	English National Leagues
	RBS Scottish Premier League
	RBS Scottish National League
	RBS Scottish Ch/ship A & B
	Welsh Principality Premiership
	Swalec pan-Wales Nat Ch/ship
	Swalec Welsh National Lges
Thu. 10th to	
Sun. 13th	Heineken Cup (5)
	Amlin Challenge Cup (5)
Fri. 11th to	
Sun. 13th	British & Irish Cup (5)
Sat. 12th	English National Leagues
	Swalec pan-Wales Nat Ch/ship
	Swalec Welsh National Lges
Thu. 17th to	
Sun. 20th	Heineken Cup (6)
	Amlin Challenge Cup (6)
Fri. 18th and	
Sat. 19th	UB Irish Leagues 2A/B
Sat. 19th	English National Leagues
	Swalec pan-Wales Nat Ch/ship
Fri. 25th to	
Sun. 27th	LV= (Anglo-Welsh) Cup (3)
	English National Championship
Sat. 26th	English National Leagues
	RBS Scottish Premier League
	RBS Scottish National League
	RBS Scottish Ch/ship A & B
	Swalec Welsh National Lges
	Swalec Cup (2)
	UB Irish Leagues 1A/B, 2A/B

FEBRUARY 2013

Fri. 1st to	
Sun. 3rd	LV= (Anglo-Welsh) Cup (4)
Sat. 2nd	WALES v IRELAND (13:30)
	ENGLAND v SCOTLAND (16:00)
	English National Leagues 1/2
Sun. 3rd	ITALY v FRANCE (15:00)
Fri. 8th to	
Sun. 10th	Aviva English Premiership (14)
	RaboDirect PRO12 (14)
	Welsh Principality Premiership
Sat. 9th	SCOTLAND v ITALY (14:30)
	FRANCE v WALES (17:00)
	English National Leagues 3
Sat. 9th and	
Sun. 10th	English National Championship
Sun. 10th	IRELAND v ENGLAND (15:00)
Fri. 15th and	
Sat. 16th	UB Irish Leagues 1A/B, 2A/B
Fri. 15th to	
Sun. 17th	Aviva English Premiership (15)
	RaboDirect PRO12 (15)
	English National Championship
Sat. 16th	English National Leagues
	RBS Scottish Premier League
	RBS Scottish National League
	RBS Scottish Ch/ship A & B

	Swalec pan-Wales Nat Ch/ship
	Swalec Welsh National Lges
	Swalec Cup (3)
Fri. 22nd and	
Sat. 23rd	UB Irish Leagues 1A/B, 2A/B
Fri. 22nd to	
Sun. 24th	Aviva English Premiership (16)
	RaboDirect PRO12 (16)
Sat. 23rd	ITALY v WALES (14:30)
	ENGLAND v FRANCE (17:00)
	RBS Scottish Premier League
	RBS Scottish National League
	RBS Scottish Ch/ship A & B
	Welsh Principality Premiership
Sun. 24th	SCOTLAND v IRELAND (14:00)

MARCH 2013

Fri. 1st and	
Sat. 2nd	UB Irish Leagues 1A/B, 2A/B
Fri. 1st to	
Sun. 3rd	Aviva English Premiership (17)
	RaboDirect PRO12 (17)
Sat. 2nd	English National Leagues
	RBS Scottish Cup QF
	RBS Scottish Shield QF
	RBS Scottish Bowl QF
	Welsh Principality Premiership
	Swalec pan-Wales Nat Ch/ship
	Swalec Welsh National Lges
Sat. 2nd and	
Sun. 3rd	English National Championship
Fri. 8th to	
Sun. 10th	English National Championship
	LV= (Anglo-Welsh) Cup SF•
Sat. 9th	SCOTLAND v WALES (14:30)
	IRELAND v FRANCE (17:00)
	English National Leagues
	Welsh Principality Premiership
Sun. 10th	ENGLAND v ITALY (15:00)
Wed. 13th	Swalec pan-Wales Nat Ch/ship
Fri. 15th to	
Sun. 17th	LV= (Anglo-Welsh) Cup Final•
Sat. 16th	ITALY v IRELAND (14:30)
	WALES v ENGLAND (17:00)
	FRANCE v SCOTLAND (20:00)
	UB Irish Leagues 1A/B
Fri. 22nd and	
Sat. 23rd	English National Championship
	UB Irish Leagues 1A/B, 2A/B
Fri. 22nd to	
Sun. 24th	Aviva English Premiership (18)
	RaboDirect PRO12 (18)
Sat. 23rd	English National Leagues
	RBS Scottish Premier League
	RBS Scottish National League
	RBS Scottish Ch/ship A & B
	Swalec pan-Wales Nat Ch/ship
	Swalec Welsh National Lges
	Swalec Cup QF
	BUCS Finals (Twickenham)
Sun. 24th	Daily Mail RBS Schools' Day
Fri. 29th and	

Sat. 30th	UB Irish Leagues 1A/B, 2A/B
Fri. 29th to Sun. 31st	Aviva English Premiership (19) RaboDirect PRO12 (19) English National Championship
Sat. 30th	English National Leagues 1/2 RBS Scottish Cup SF RBS Scottish Shield SF RBS Scottish Bowl SF Welsh Principality Premiership Swalec pan-Wales Nat Ch/ship Swalec Welsh National Lges

APRIL 2013

Thu. 4th to Sun. 7th	Heineken Cup QF Amlin Challenge Cup QF
Sat. 6th	English National Leagues RBS Scottish Premier League Play-off Swalec pan-Wales Nat Ch/ship Swalec Welsh National Lges
Fri. 12th and Sat. 13th	UB Irish Leagues 1A/B, 2A/B
Fri. 12th to Sun. 14th	Aviva English Premiership (20) RaboDirect PRO12 (20)
Sat. 13th	English National Leagues Swalec pan-Wales Nat Ch/ship Swalec Welsh National Lges Swalec Cup SF
Sat. 13th and Sun. 14th	English National Championship
Fri. 19th to Sun. 21st	Aviva English Premiership (21) RaboDirect PRO12 (21)
Sat. 20th	St George's Day Game (Twickenham) English National Championship English National Leagues RBS Scottish Cup Final RBS Scottish Shield Final RBS Scottish Bowl Final Welsh Principality Premiership Swalec pan-Wales Nat Ch/ship Swalec Welsh National Lges UB Irish Leagues 1A/B National U20 Ch/ship SF
Thu. 25th to Sun. 28th	Heineken Cup SF• Amlin Challenge Cup SF• British & Irish Cup SF•

Sat. 27th	Army v Navy
	Combined Services U23
	    v Oxbridge U23
	        (both Twickenham)
	English National Leagues 1/2
	English National Leagues 3 and
	    Divisional Play-offs
	Welsh Principality Premiership

Mon. 29th	Aviva 'A' League Final

MAY 2013

Fri. 3rd to Sun. 5th	Aviva English Premiership (22) RaboDirect PRO12 (22)

Sat. 4th	English National Championship
	    Play-off SF (1)
	English National Leagues 1/2
	    Play-offs
	RFU Intermediate Cup Final
	RFU Senior Vase Final
	RFU Junior Vase Final
	National U20 Ch/ship Final
	Swalec Cup Final

Sat. 4th and Sun. 5th	HSBC 7s WS Round 9 (Glasgow)

Sat. 11th	English National Championship
	    Play-off SF (2)
	Welsh Principality Premiership
	    Play-off SF

Sat. 11th and Sun. 12th	HSBC 7s WS Round 10 (London) Aviva English Premiership SF RaboDirect PRO12 SF•
Fri. 17th	Amlin Challenge Cup Final
Fri. 17th to Sun. 19th	British & Irish Cup Final•
Sat. 18th	Heineken Cup Final
Thu. 23rd	English National Championship Play-off Final (1)

Sat. 25th	Aviva English Premiership Final
	RaboDirect PRO12 Final•
	County Championship
	    (Bill Beaumont Cup) Final
	County Ch/ship Shield Final
	Welsh Principality Premiership
	    Play-off Final

Sun. 26th	England v Barbarians
Wed. 29th	English National Championship Play-off Final (2)

Key
RC = Rugby Championship, successor
competition to the Tri-Nations
• indicates dates and times to be confirmed

JUNE/JULY 2013
British & Irish Lions Tour to Australia

Sat.	1st June	v Barbarians (Hong Kong)
Wed.	5th	v Western Force (Perth)
Sat.	8th	v Queensland Reds (Brisbane)
Wed.	12th	v Combined NSW/Queensland Country (Newcastle)
Sat.	15th	v NSW Waratahs (Sydney)
Tue.	18th	v ACT Brumbies (Canberra)
Sat.	22nd	v AUSTRALIA (Brisbane)
Tue.	25th	v Melbourne Rebels (Melbourne)
Sat.	29th	v AUSTRALIA (Melbourne)
Sat.	6th July	v AUSTRALIA (Sydney)